Women

of the

Upper Class

Susan A. Ostrander

TEMPLE UNIVERSITY PRESS
PHILADELPHIA

Temple University Press, Philadelphia 19122
© 1984 by Temple University. All rights reserved
Published 1984
Printed in the United States of America

Library of Congress Cataloging in Publication Data

Ostrander, Susan A.
    Women of the upper class.

    (Women in the political economy)
    Bibliography: p.
    Includes index.
    1. Upper classes—United States—Case studies.
2. Married women—United States— Case studies.
I. Title. II. Series.
HT653.U6087 1984   305.4   83-18214
ISBN 0-87722-334-3

To my son Mark and to John—for
all the reasons authors dedicate
books to those who live with them
day to day

Contents

Acknowledgments

The person who has been most intimately involved in the preparation of the final draft of this book is the series editor, Ronnie Steinberg. Her warm support, wisdom, and force of intellect have greatly improved this work. I am immensely grateful to her. Michael Ames at Temple University Press also deserves a special thanks for his willingness to take a chance on a new author and an unfinished work.

Bill Domhoff has been a consistent and strong supporter of my work since we met on a professional panel several years ago. He edited the draft that led to a publication contract, and he never doubted that this book would become a reality. His ongoing attention, interest, and advice are the stuff of which young scholars are made. I thank Bill for his continued support and encouragement.

Several others read an earlier draft of the manuscript and made critically important suggestions for its improvement. Though they did not always agree on what the final version should look like, they all urged me to press on. Carol Brown, Roslyn Feldberg, and Nona Glazer gave me the kind of close and detailed comments an author needs to bring a work to fruition. I thank Nona especially for referring me to the work of Dorothy Smith. Paula Raymon put in a good word at the right time. My colleague Mary Jane Cramer called my attention to Gidden's concept of meaning. Arlene Daniels swooped in on several occasions when my spirits were flagging and brought me back up. She sent me a thoughtful critique, and she urged me to seek the advice of others. Perhaps most important, she shared with me drafts of her own work. Jessie Bernard appeared when I was at a particularly low point. Her reading of the manuscript and her fresh encouragement were a genuine turning point for which I am most appreciative.

In the earliest stages of the study, I enjoyed the guidance and unwavering support of my professors Irwin Deutscher, Marie Haug, and Jetse Sprey. They were my first advisors, without whom the work would have never begun.

I was fortunate that all of the people who typed the several drafts did so much more than type. Peg McCarthy, Sandy Ennis, Maureen DeVito, and Juanita Nicholson, were genuine colleagues. They raised questions and made suggestions that led to a better book. I am grateful for their patience, their speed, and their level of interest and encouragement, which went far beyond what was required.

Finally, I wish to thank the women who allowed me to interview them for this study. Without them, there would be no book.

Susan A. Ostrander
Tufts University
Medford, MA
June 1983

Women of the Upper Class

Introduction:
The
Upper-Class
Woman

1

Contrary to popular belief, the life of the upper-class woman is not all champagne and roses, trips to Paris and Palm Beach. The upper-class woman is also not very interested in high fashion, nor is she a jet-setting party-goer. Her days are not spent lying around the country club pool or attending elegant ladies' luncheons. Though she certainly lives in far greater luxury than women—or men—of any other class, she is no lady of leisure, no spoiled and pampered grand dame. She is, rather, an active and important member of community service and arts boards, an involved and dedicated mother, and a devoted, subservient wife. In short, she is a hard-working member of society; though, as this study suggests, her work serves largely to uphold the power and privilege of her own class in the social order of things.

This study describes the day-to-day *activities* of upper-class women, with an emphasis on their *meaning* and *consequence*. It examines what these activities mean for the women themselves and explores the consequences these activities have for maintaining the upper class. The subjects of this study belong to the wealthiest, most powerful and socially prominent class in American society. I show how their activities are essential to maintaining this class. Further, I demonstrate that their activities are given meaning within a class framework that they themselves construct, and that this framework creates and perpetuates the social-organizational forms and patterns of cultural life necessary to class domination.[1] "Meaning" is defined here as the institutional framework(s) that subjects use to make sense of their daily activities: in this case, the frameworks are class and gender.[2] "Meaning" is not being used in the sense of intent and purpose, nor as a subjective category (since the institutional frameworks that give meaning are objectively real though created and maintained by subjects).

Thirty-six upper-class women were interviewed for this study. The descriptions of their everyday activities and their meaning are presented here as they were presented to me—grouped into the social roles of wife, mother, club member, and community volunteer. Beyond these descriptions, the consequences of the women's activities for upholding the position of the upper class are necessarily a matter of interpretation. My interpretations and explanations are intended to be plausible and suggestive rather than conclusive. Since this is the first study to focus on women of the upper class, it is frankly and appropriately exploratory.

It is important to establish from the outset an objective definition of "upper class."[3] When people in the United States think of class, they usually think first of money. The class they belong to generally depends on the kind of work they do, the income they earn, and their education. For the upper class, the definition of "class" goes well beyond income, occupation, and education—factors used by social scientists and the general populace alike to determine social class. For the upper class, the most important factors

are the ownership of wealth, the exercise of power, and membership in an exclusive social network.

E. Digby Baltzell has argued that the primary characteristic
of the upper class is the exercise of power in society.[4] This power
derives largely from the concentrated ownership of personal wealth
and ownership of the economic forces that produce the goods and
services upon which we all depend. The American upper class,
estimated to comprise only one percent of the population,[5] owns
half of all the corporate stock in the United States[6] and one fifth of
the national wealth (real estate and other property, cash, bonds, and
insurance).[7] G. William Domhoff concludes that the upper class
"controls major banks and corporations, formulates economic and
political programs through a series of policy networks, and domi-
nates . . . the federal government in Washington."[8] In addition to
economic and political aspects—the ownership of wealth and the
exercise of power—the social aspect is an important definitional
characteristic of the upper class. Some social scientists, following
Weber, would call this "status" instead of class. Baltzell focuses on
this aspect of the upper class, claiming that it provides the social
supports for the exercise of power. He defines the upper class as:

> a group of families whose members are descendants of suc-
> cessful individuals of one, two, three or more generations
> ago . . . the top of the social class hierarchy. They are brought
> up together and they are friends. They intermarry and have
> a distinctive style of life. There is a primary group solidarity
> that sets them apart from the rest of the population.[9]

In conceptual terms then, "upper class" is defined here as that
portion of the population that owns the major share of corporate
and personal wealth, exercises dominant power in economic and
political affairs, and comprises exclusive social networks and organizations open only to persons born into or selected by this class.

Class-exclusive organizations are useful in identifying and

studying individual members of the upper class. In other words, membership in exclusive organizations distinguishes persons who are upper class from those who are not. The social registers of certain cities and specific social clubs and secondary schools have been designated by Baltzell, Domhoff, and others as indicative of upper-class membership. Domhoff has developed lists of such clubs (such as the Pacific Union club in San Francisco and the Knickerbocker club in New York), private secondary schools (such as Groton in Massachusetts and Rosemary Hall in Connecticut), and social registers (of cities such as Boston, New York, Pittsburgh, Baltimore, and St. Louis).[10]

Except for Domhoff and Baltzell, social scientists have conducted very few studies of the upper class, and those studies do not focus on the women of this class. When the women are mentioned, it is most often in relation to their husbands and their family role. Some four decades ago, Warner and Lunt stated in their studies of the class structure of Yankee City that "the upper class woman participated in the society—primarily as the wife of her husband."[11] In the early sixties, Baltzell did work that refers to the role of upper-class women in maintaining the family.[12] Studies of the upper-class family have found rigid gender differentiation and gender stratification. Blood and Wolfe reported in 1960 that the division of labor among upper-class husbands and wives was more rigid than among wives and husbands of other social classes.[13] Helen Hacker and Clarice Stasz (Stoll), drawing primarily from other studies, report similar findings; and Hacker concludes that "the upper class husband has greater marital power than husbands in other social classes."[14] Paul Blumberg, in a replication of a 1947 study by Hatch and Hatch, found striking stability in the upper-class family compared to families in other classes.[15]

Very little social science literature calls attention to the upper-class woman's community work, which consists primarily of serving on the boards of cultural organizations (such as symphony orchestras and art museums), colleges and universities, health-related organizations (primarily hospitals), and charitable and social welfare organizations.[16] Theodore Caplow, in a text on the sociology of work published in 1954, noted the importance among upper-class women of the substitution of volunteer work in the community for gainful employment. Caplow's study, like the present study, emphasizes the extent to which volunteer work maintains the upper class itself.[17] Sociologist Joan Moore conducted a study over twenty years ago of women's participation on the boards of metropolitan hospitals. She found that upper-class women (rather than middle-class women) were more likely to move rapidly into positions of leadership on the boards. Moore attributed this to the fact that these women were descendants of the families who had founded the hospitals. She concluded that board work had a different meaning for the upper-class women than for the middle-class women, stating that ". . . for the upper class [board membership] plays a role of significance for the entire class."[18] In a study of housewives reported in 1971, Helena Lopata found that only upper-class wives listed "obligation to society" as their top priority in community volunteer work.[19]

In a more recent study, Ann Tickamyer suggests that, although upper-class women may be active in community affairs, they participate no more than men of their class, and they have not achieved positions of national prominence.[20] Except for Moore's and Tickamyer's studies, all these works make no more than brief mention of the women of the upper class. Moore's work was done over two decades ago. Tickamyer's work is based solely on *Who's Who* listings of eighteen women listed in *Fortune* as among the wealthiest individuals in America. While the work raises an important question about the relative influence of the men and women of the upper class, the use of great wealth as the only criterion for upper-class membership is questionable, and the limitations of the sources for gauging community participation are considerable.

The most extensive mention of these women in recent social science literature is a chapter in Domhoff's work, *The Higher Circles,* entitled "The Feminine Half of the Upper Class." Using historical, biographical, and documentary sources—such as Junior League publications and the reports of newspaper "Society" editors—Domhoff formulates the role of upper-class women as follows:

> First, they are the mistresses of the social institutions that keep this collection of rich families an intermarrying social class. In other words, they are the gatekeepers and caretakers of upper class societal institutions. They provide the framework within which the members of the class get to know one another. A second function of women of the upper class is the setting of social and cultural standards for the rest of the population to admire and emulate. [The third function] is involvement in welfare movements which attempt to improve the lot of the general population. In blunt language, women of the upper class serve an important function by helping to take some of the roughest edges off a profit-oriented system that has cared little for specific human needs.[21]

Domhoff urges others to look further into the function of the roles of upper-class women.

In summary, previous research on upper-class women is very scarce; the little work that does exist looks at these women in relation to their families and to their husbands; and, for the most part, only cursory attention has been paid to the importance of their work in the community. Virtually no one, with the exception of Domhoff, has mentioned their role in creating an overall social and cultural context for upper-class life. No one has shown how the activities of upper-class women are essential to maintain the power and privilege of the class; and no one has derived data primarily from interviews with upper-class women. This is the contribution and importance of the present study.

Methodology

The women interviewed for this study are members of the upper-class. They belong to clubs listed by Domhoff for the city in which this study was conducted, and they are listed in the social register or have attended the upper-class schools listed by Domhoff (either eastern boarding schools or local day schools). These are very conservative criteria: they leave out, for example, the Junior League and clubs listed by society editors and other journalists, such as Lucy Kaveler and Cleveland Amory, who have studied the upper class.[22] Domhoff considers that any one of these three criteria—social register, club, or school—is sufficient for membership in the upper class. Most of the women interviewed (22 out of 36) met two or more of the three criteria. (See Appendix A for the demographic characteristics of the 36 subjects of this study. All of the names are fictitious, and the women are listed in the order in which they were interviewed.)

I met the women interviewed through what is known in the social sciences as the "snowball" method: that is, each subject introduced me to one or more other women. At the conclusion of each interview, I asked the woman to "suggest another woman of your social group with a background like yours who might be willing to talk with me." This practical way of gaining access to respondents had theoretical as well as methodological advantages. I am now able to say that the objective criteria used by social scientists to identify upper-class people—social register, clubs, and schools—are consistent with those used by upper-class persons themselves. Since I was using this particular method to obtain a group of women to talk to, the first woman interviewed was very important in setting the "snowball" off on the right track. She needed to be able to tell me how to contact others and how to present the study to them so that they would want to participate. She also contributed to the early identification of specific issues for study. She had to be an objectively identifiable member of the upper class; but it was preferable that she be somewhat marginal to this class, so that she might be sympathetic to the study's focus on class maintenance.[23] It was only at the conclusion of the research process that I realized how difficult it should have been to find such a person. Fortunately, I met Mrs. Wainwright by chance through an academic colleague who knew her from work on a community project. She was immediately receptive and enthusiastic about participating, and she met every one of the criteria listed above. She knew the elderly women from the oldest families, who were essential to my "getting in." And she advised me, "It's important for you to go in the right order. You have to start at the top."

By way of introducing my study, I appealed to the subjects specifically as women. I suggested that, while we know a good deal about the men from old and influential families, we know little about the women. This approach proved successful. I know of only two women who were unwilling to talk with me, pleading busy schedules.

Though I knew the kinds of issues I wanted to discuss with the women, my questions were open-ended and the issues became more focused as the study progressed.[24] I wanted to find out, first, what life activities were important to them. I did this by beginning the early interviews with the broadest of questions, such as what they did on a typical day. Since the women divided their activities into activities inside and outside the home, I then began asking questions in those terms. Eventually my questions focused on the four roles the women used to organize their lives—wife, mother, club member, and community volunteer. This book is organized around those roles.

After discovering the women's primary life activities, I wanted to know what kind of meaning framework—primarily class or gender contexts—they used to make sense of these activities. For example, I asked initially about the kinds of activities they were involved in outside the home. Whatever activities they then discussed, I asked what it meant to them *personally* to be involved in such activities and what *social* contribution such activities made. If their responses to such questions were almost entirely in terms of their upper-class social position—such as the obligation of this class to contribute to the community through volunteer work—I concluded that the class context was of primary importance to them in regard to their volunteer work. I also noted what kinds of explanations the women spontaneously gave for life events, such as explaining a son's failed marriage on the basis of class incompatibility. It is important to note here that, although this study begins in Chapter 2 with a discussion of what class means to the women, I did not raise the issue of class explicitly until the *end* of the interview, when subjects were asked what it meant to them to belong to their social group and its advantages and disadvantages. Thus, it cannot be said that the women's use of class contexts was influenced significantly by the research itself. (The three interview schedules used at various stages of this study can be found in Appendix B. Interviews were generally of about two hours in length.)

There are, of course, a number of limitations to the methodology. One is the matter of generalizing the conclusions to upper-class women overall. This is always a concern where the sampling method is less than systematically random. But, while it cannot be ignored, it seems no more serious here than in other qualitative studies with a small sample of respondents. Though a larger sample is of some advantage in arguing representativeness, I chose to use thirty-six women, following the sampling principle posed by Glaser and Straus.[25] That is, I was getting no new data that it seemed would significantly alter my analysis. It is also true—in regard to the issue of generalizability—that I was referred to women who were considered by their class peers to be representative of the class; thus, I did not speak with women who deviated significantly from the norms of upper-class life. But I was most interested in "acceptable" people, since I wanted to learn the established norms and definitions of "acceptable." Further, given the way I constructed my sample, I have no reason to believe that it is an isolated pocket of the upper class. Though the women did, by definition, travel in the same social circles, they did not all know one another, nor did they all view one another with equanimity. They were people with national connections: they had summer homes in other parts of the country and often sent their children to schools away from home. They traveled frequently, and some belonged to clubs in other cities.

The sample is "biased" in one sense—it contains only married women presently living with their husbands or elderly women recently widowed. This is because I wanted to investigate the role of upper-class women in their families, in their class roles as wives and mothers. Consequently, the women I spoke with may be especially traditional, and they are not the single mavericks of upper-class life. Another seeming limitation of this study is the fact that— as with all studies using interviews as the sole source of information—I can only report what my subjects told me. I can only describe the social and cultural context that these women create—and that, once created, serves to define and give meaning to their own lives and to maintain their class—only to the extent that they were willing and able to tell me about it.

This study was conducted in a midwestern city, one of the ten largest in the country, with a metropolitan population of over two million. Founded in the early 1800s, it has an upper class dating back to the nineteenth century. The city is a national industrial and management center, and over forty corporations have their headquarters there. The women interviewed range in age from their mid-thirties to their mid-eighties. They were all married, though three are widowed; and most of the women are descendants of the city's oldest families. A few of the women (4) are "newcomers." These women had moved to the city, some as long as twenty years ago. They belong to the "right" clubs, and their children go to the "right" schools; but they are not "well-born."

All of the women but two have children; the majority have

three or more. Their husbands are generally in business or corporate law. Nearly a third of the husbands (13) are presidents or chairmen of boards; about one quarter of them (8) are presidents of old family firms; and two of the husbands are physicians. [All but five of the women have a college education.] (Those who do not tend to be the older women in the sample.) Nearly half of the college-educated women had attended Vassar, Smith, or Wellesley; and half of the husbands had attended Harvard, Yale, or Princeton. One of the women has a full-time paying job, and one has a part-time paying job. Nearly all belong to the Junior League, and many belong to a Garden Club. Although all of the women share an upper-class identity—and the focus in this study is what they have in common—there is variation among the individuals. Let me introduce some of the individual women as they were on the day we met.

Meeting the Women

Mrs. Smythe is an elegant woman in her late forties. She is from one of the city's oldest families. As she was nearly twenty minutes late for our interview (having come from a luncheon for the city's opera society), I was able to make some observations of her home. The first thing that struck me about the urban mansion was a large indoor pool surrounded by billowing draperies. It was a scene reminiscent of Fitzgerald's *Great Gatsby*. A West Indian maid in uniform ushered me into a small sunroom off the entranceway. Several magazines and journals—*Architectual Design, Historic Preservation, Antiques, Time, The New Yorker*, the *Harvard Review*—lay around the room. There were a few family photographs, a collection of china cups and saucers, a cart with various liqueurs, decanters, and an empty club soda bottle. No television or books were in evidence; only a small, portable f.m. radio sat on the floor next to a chair. Mrs. Smythe is listed in the social register and belongs to the city's oldest and most prestigious country club. She attended an upper-class boarding school in the eastern part of the country, and her daughter now attends the same school. She is a member of the Junior League, like nearly all of the women in this study, and is an active and highly respected community volunteer, who describes herself as "a deep believer in volunteerism."

Mrs. Ames is also from an old family. She is an attractive woman in her sixties, whose short white hair and handcrafted gold jewelry were shown to advantage on a becoming tan (though it was late September in a city not known for its hours of bright sun). Mrs. Ames' home is very different from that of the Smythes. Located in the country, it can only be found with the help of precise directions and a careful description of the stone gate, the only evidence that a house is nearby. The driveway turns through landscaped fields, where several gardeners can be seen at work. The house is modern, mostly glass and wood. An independent woman, Mrs. Ames has tired of volunteer work, saying that she "had done all the good works" and "really had to discover . . . what I did best." In recent years, she has become a serious artist and the house is filled with her work. Though she is listed in the social register and her children attend upper-class schools, she does not belong to the city's most elite club, preferring instead a slightly newer club considered locally to be very prestigious. Her husband, like many upper-class men of his generation, heads an old family firm.

Mrs. Sharpe, on the other hand, is heavily involved in community affairs. The patio where we met was chaotic, with piles of mail everywhere. Mrs. Sharpe, a woman in her sixties, is a robust, no-nonsense person. Her style is not a warm one. She took charge immediately, greeting me with, "I suppose you want me to tell you all about my family and all the things they've done for the city." She apologized briefly for the mess, saying that she was in the middle of organizing an immense fundraising dinner and was "terrified" because she was using a new caterer. Mrs. Sharpe is listed in the social register, as were her parents. She belongs to the most elite club and, of course, the Junior League. Her husband "deals in stocks."

Mrs. Hoight, a woman in her late forties, is also very involved in community work, though she is somewhat more modest about it than Mrs. Sharpe. She lives in a comparatively simple colonial home in a planned private community. I am greeted here, as in several other homes, by a large hunting dog. Mrs. Hoight was on the telephone when I arrived, and it rang several times during our interview, always related to one of her community activities. Mrs. Hoight is tan and rugged looking. She has very short, grey-blond hair and was dressed in work jeans with a man's shirt hanging out. She served strong coffee in large cups and dealt with my questions in a quick, businesslike manner. Mrs. Hoight is married to an independent investment consultant—a common occupation for upper-class men—which often appeared to be a euphemism for working full-time to manage the family money. She said that her husband wished she would "stay home more than I do." She is listed in the social register, as are her parents, and her children attend local upper-class day schools.

Mrs. Clarke is one of the younger women I spoke with. She is in her thirties, and her two-and-a-half-year-old child napped as we talked. She and her husband have two other sons who are currently attending the local upper-class day school. Her husband is from a somewhat more prominent family, though her parents are also listed in the social register along with herself and her husband. Mr. Clarke had recently been made a full partner in the old family law firm, and he feels he has to work very hard to prove himself. (Apparently there had been some question as to whether he would be made a partner. The Clarkes had talked about what they would do if he were not and had decided they would have left the city.) Mrs. Clarke is somewhat lonely. She feels isolated with her young child, and her husband is rarely home. She has "almost no help, just a girl who comes in every day from three to six. . . . [who]

cleans and helps me with dinner." It seems that there are some money problems. She said that her husband is "feeling broke." She would like to have more money. But then she would have to provide it herself, and she would rather have her money to spend on other things. Mrs. Clarke is on the boards of a local health clinic and the city's art association. She doesn't want to follow the pattern of her mother-in-law, who is very active in the community, but she doesn't know what else she wants to do.

Mrs. Haines is somewhat younger than Mrs. Clarke. When I arrived in her relatively small white house on the main street of a little village outside the city—a village considered locally to be a very exclusive place to live—she and a friend were addressing envelopes for a benefit for the city's symphony orchestra. Mrs. Haines is a lovely, and bouncy young woman. She was dressed in a navy blue sweater, white blouse with a round collar, and plaid wool slacks, with a velvet band in her sandy hair. Like Mrs. Clarke, she had married into a family older than her own, and she is not listed in the social register though her husband's parents are. She and her husband do belong to the top country club, which is located not far from their house. He is a corporate lawyer, and she said that during their eight years of marriage he has usually been away from home five days a week. They have two children, ages four and six, and "a girl" who comes in three days a week to help. Like Mrs. Clarke, Mrs. Haines doesn't see herself doing volunteer work all her life, and she mentioned the possibility of going back to school in art history.

Mrs. Atherton, an attractive woman in her fifties, is a "newcomer" to the city. Her husband heads an old firm. They are already in the social register and belong to the most elite upper-class clubs. She left me briefly in "the library," saying that she had something to finish upstairs. Someone was working in the house, and Mrs. Atherton gave instructions about how the beds were to be made up. Unlike women from the old families, Mrs. Atherton spoke of how important it is for her to support her husband's position in the community by doing volunteer work and business entertaining. The other women do not think their husbands need this kind of support, as they are already well established. Mrs. Atherton was also more open than the others about what she sees as the dark side of upper-class life. She said that the tensions of living at the top result in drinking problems, that the frequent moves of corporate executives take a heavy toll on the women and children, and that family problems are not acknowledged or discussed. She also described the process that she and her husband had gone through to "get in," and the need to enhance their position in the community so they would be sponsored and accepted into the upper-class social networks. She sees her own role in life primarily as being supportive to her husband, and her work on the boards of the symphony, the opera association, and the city playhouse are part of that role. Yet she is an independent woman who, although centering her life around her husband, does not kowtow to him.

Mrs. Hammond is also a relative newcomer to the city. She and her husband, who heads a very large and well-known international firm, have lived here for twenty years. He is often in the news for his local work with the United Way. They are not yet in the social register, though their daughter, Mrs. Carnes, is. They do belong to the top clubs. Their five children all have attended upper-class schools, either the local day schools or elite eastern boarding schools. When they first arrived in the city, Mrs. Hammond claims that she often worked forty-hour weeks doing volunteer work through the Junior League. Since they were not city "natives," it "was a way to get to know people," similar to what Mrs. Atherton had said about the need to work to become accepted. Also, like Mrs. Atherton, Mrs. Hammond defined herself as an important support to her husband's business position. At a time when he was out of the country for the better part of five years, she took complete charge of their household and five children. "That's just a woman's job," she said.

Mrs. Hall, like most of the women I spoke with, is from

one of the very oldest families in the city. She is in her forties. As we sat by a pool outside her ultramodern home, she pointed to a huge white house far in the distance, up on a hill. Her father had built that house some eighty years ago, and she had been raised there. Now, she is somewhat "ashamed" of her class and was dressed almost shabbily in slacks and shirt. She said she feels "immense guilt" for all her money, and regrets the class snobbery of her earlier years. ["I really thought," she said, "that people who weren't in my class, people who weren't brought up the way I was, were different from me. I thought they were beneath me. There was no reason why I had to be civil to them, because they weren't as good as I was. You get this imbued in you."] Mrs. Hall is married to a "business consultant." She is presently at considerable odds with her husband since he opposes her desire to pursue a professional career in science. She views her years of volunteer work as largely wasted, saying that at Junior League meetings it seemed to her that "the most important thing was how neat your hat was." Mrs. Hall is listed in the social register, following her parents' tradition. She is a member of the oldest and most exclusive social club in the city, and her children attended the local upper-class day schools.

Mrs. Spears was the only woman I spoke with who has a full-time, paid career. She is an academic and the chairperson of her department. She had married into an old, nationally known political family and appeared to be particularly happy in her marriage. She said of her husband, "We have a partnership . . . and that's partly because I've always worked." Her husband is a corporate lawyer, currently out of political office. It bothers her that, when they attend social events, she is introduced simply as his wife and her own accomplishments are ignored. She has a great sense of humor, and an exuberance and energy that is most appealing. She is in the social register, and her children attended upper-class schools; but she and her husband have declined the most exclusive clubs, fearing that membership would cause resentment among his political constituency. She is one of the few women I talked with who does not belong to the Junior League, citing her professional work as the reason.

These brief vignettes show that the women I interviewed are quite diverse as individuals. They are of different ages, and they are from both the new and old branches of the upper class. They represent various lifestyles and outlooks, within the boundaries of upper-class life. Though all—including Mrs. Spears, who has a full-time, paid professional career—are involved in volunteer work, they have somewhat different views of their commitment to it and of its importance to their husbands' positions. The amount of household help they have varies, though all have some. Their children attend boarding schools or local day schools. Some of the women are happier in their marriages and lives than others. Some, like Mrs. Atherton and Mrs. Hammond, see themselves as part of a team with their husbands, contributing significantly to the men's positions in the business world. Others, like Mrs. Hall, feel at odds with their husbands and see their wifely responsibilities as obstacles to what they want to do with their own lives. For a few, like Mrs. Clarke, there is not enough money to maintain the life to which they are accustomed, and this causes a strain. Some live in homes that exude great wealth, like Mrs. Smythe; others, like Mrs. Hoight, live in homes that—while certainly far beyond what most people could afford—are not appreciably different from the homes of successful upper-middle-class doctors, lawyers, or business executives.

The differences among these women are, for the most part, idiosyncratic and do not have constant patterns. The similarities of how they live and define their lives seem to far outweigh the differences, with two exceptions. The exceptions—differences that do seem to have a pattern—are variances between the newcomers and the old families, and a few differences by age. "Newcomers," as they called themselves, are women not born into the oldest, "first families" of the city. Though they meet the criteria for upper-class membership—both in objective terms and in terms of being referred by old-family women—they generally feel they will never be as fully accepted into the upper class as the old families. This results in a number of differences in experience, such as the importance of business entertaining and the importance of the wife's community activities in enhancing her husband's position. In terms of age, there is a slight tendency among the younger women to want to pursue paid, professional careers. Mrs. Carnes has a temporary, part-time paid job in public relations; Mrs. Howe talked about the possibility of law school, and Mrs. Haines, of art history. But older women also had professional interests, thus defying any real consistency in age patterns. Mrs. Hall wanted to become a professional scientist, Mrs. Spears had worked as an academic most of her life, Mrs. Ames had taken to independent artistry, and Mrs. Wainwright was pursuing an advanced social science degree. Besides paid work, the younger women also seemed no more likely than older ones to respond to other trends of the women's movement such as a change in household division of labor. A number of the women were somewhat up in arms about the subordination of women, but they were as likely to be older women (like Mrs. Hall and Mrs. Wilson), as they were to be younger ones (like Mrs. Howe).

Since the differences within the group of women did not seem to be considerable, I have concentrated on the similarities. As this is the first study to focus on women of the upper class, I have defined and analyzed the *commonalities* of their way of life; later studies may find it appropriate to look further for the differences within this defined pattern.

The
Meaning
of
Upper
Class

2

In social science literature and in popular belief, it is often suggested that socioeconomic class is of little interest or importance to people in everyday life in the United States. Studies of class consciousness often conclude that they are not particularly aware of the importance of class position, nor do they live or define their lives within class contexts.[1] Socioeconomic classes are seen as not entirely real for Americans, except as constructs for social scientific analysis.[2]

I expected, therefore, that it might be difficult to interview specific respondents about the meaning of their socioeconomic position—even knowing that studies have also shown the upper class and upper-class women, in particular, to be the most class-conscious segment of the American population.[3] I need not have worried. The women I interviewed spoke easily and articulately about the upper class and how it frames their lives. Furthermore, the ways they defined and described their class were quite different from the ways social scientists typically study class in American society. These conversations thus provided insights into the concept of class as it is experienced by upper-class people in everyday life—and they set the scene for the remainder of this study.

Personal meanings

Social scientists often use measures of occupation, income, and education to assess class position and to study social class in society. The social class of a woman is most frequently established by her husband's position according to these measures.[4] For the upper-class women with whom I spoke, however, these dimensions of socioeconomic class had little meaning. When they spontaneously spoke of themselves or others as members of the upper class and in relation to the community, they rarely spoke of income, education, or their husbands' occupations. The few women who did speak of these matters were the exceptions.

Mrs. Bennett, for example, described the meaning of upper class as being the "head of big [business] concerns." Mrs. Hoight (whose husband is an independent management consultant with his office in their home) said, "Social class is a certain income level, a certain education, and a prominent position in the community in terms of what your husband does." Mrs. Harper (whose husband is a partner in one of the oldest law firms in the city) said: "We're successful people, people at my income level. My husband's father was considered to be one of the top lawyers in the city." Mrs. Appleton (whose husband heads a firm that he inherited from his family) called the term upper class a "snob term," but went on to say, "If it's used realistically in terms of income, I guess it's alright."

To these women, who rarely have paid occupations from which to derive an independent class identity, the husband's position is not of much importance. Certainly, upper-class men must continue to have well-paying and high positions in, for instance, business or corporate law in order to exercise economic power; but those positions are not considered to be major criteria for class membership. They are the taken-for-granted consequence of other more salient characteristics. How, then, do upper-class women define themselves and their class?

First of all, according to the women interviewed, people are *born* into the upper class. The importance of birthright was evident when the women chose other subjects for me to talk with. The appropriate subjects were considered to be class equals. They were chosen on the basis of their family names and lineages, and by virtue of the contributions made by their parents and grandparents to the community. When the women talked about the meaning of class, they mentioned their ancestry, heritage, and breeding—of "being from an old line family" or "being born like we are." Mrs. Wainwright, for example, was told she was "well born": "Mother didn't mean well born in America. She meant before you got here from Europe—landed aristocracy."

Many of the women spoke with pride of their ancestors who had been founders of the city: streets, parks, buildings, and institutions in the arts, social services, and education carried their names. They sometimes mentioned what generation they were, often fourth or fifth. Mrs. Martin spoke of her concern that the old families were being outnumbered, that her social circle included people who were not city natives: "My mother and grandmother were born here, so was my father and his father. There aren't so many of us anymore. Today you run into so many people who were born in other cities."

But what about those members of the upper class who are not of the oldest stock—those who belong to the right clubs, go to the right schools, and eventually get themselves or their children listed in the local social register, but are not from the first families? Upper-class "newcomers" have often moved to a particular city

23

from another geographical area. Less frequently, they are carefully selected members of families of new wealth and power who are brought into upper-class social circles. Mrs. Nesbitt, for example, has ostensibly been completely accepted by the community's old upper class since her move from another city. She is a woman in her sixties whose husband heads a large national firm. She and her husband are listed in the social register, and they are members of the oldest and most exclusive club. She said however: "[The old families] will always look at me as an outsider. They've been very kind in their way, but I'll always be an outsider. They've always gone with the same people, and they talk about people I don't know. Their lives are ingrown."

Mrs. Atherton (whose husband heads the city's most prestigious accounting firm) is, like Mrs. Nesbitt, in the social register and the city's oldest club. She also has felt like an outsider since her move to town and implied that the old-line families were narrow in their social contacts: "I don't have high social standing compared to the Spears or the Brownleys. I like to associate with different groups of people. I've always felt a little strange when people start talking about people they went to school with because I don't know them. I'm not born and bred in this city."

Another "newcomer" is Mrs. Hammond, whose husband presides over a very large international corporation. They have lived in the city for twenty years. They have not yet made the city's social register; but their daughter, Mrs. Carnes, has—on her father's merits, not her husband's. They are members of the city's most elite upper-class club. Mrs. Hammond thinks that some of the old families in the city have fallen behind the times and are not living up to their responsibilities as leaders: "I think there are a great many old city families who have just gone by the boards in terms of giving. Their fathers and grandfathers were the instigators of most of what's good here, but now you have newcomers like my husband and myself who are valuable to the city. We're not old city.

It's the name my husband has made. Lots of people from the old families aren't contributing now to make a better city. You have more newcomers that really care."

Mrs. Nesbitt, too, thinks that some of the old family women have lost touch with the community's needs: "The women do their social work religiously. They think they're liberal, but they're not. They really do not relate to the problems of the inner city. They have absolutely no understanding of the problems of Blacks."

These comments might suggest the tale of the fox who couldn't reach quite high enough to get the grapes, and so decided that they weren't worth having. The newcomers' comments do, however, support the conclusion that the most important criterion for entrée into the established upper class is the family into which one is born. If one is rich enough and powerful enough for *long* enough, if one is able to acquire the appropriate manners, values, and sponsors, one may eventually gain acceptance. But this acceptance is always conditional, and one never quite achieves the social position of the first families.[5]

In addition to ancestry, the women also talked about "high social position"—in explicit recognition of a structured social hierarchy—as an indication of being upper class. They spoke of themselves as being "the upper crust," "prominent," and "of a certain strata." They used the terms "established people," "people at the top," "highly respected in the community," and "people with a certain reputation."

As evidenced from these responses, upper-class women see themselves and their class as "outstanding leaders" in the community, and deserving of the special regard in which they are held and of the rewards that follow. Mrs. Langdon, for example, spoke of "people who have contributed a great deal to the community," and Mrs. Hughes, of "responsible people."

Being born (or not) into an old first family and being part of society's uppermost stratum are social facts of upper-class life.

25

For the women I interviewed, they are meaningful facts, which provide a basis for defining the upper class in more individual, experiential ways. These more individual expressions of class in everyday life—the importance of friendships with persons of the same class, the standards of morality and propriety, the pleasures of privilege as well as the burdens—are described in the remainder of this chapter.

Many of the women defined their class as people like themselves or people they knew well. They emphasized a homogenous outlook and established patterns of association. They talked about "my personal friends," "families I've known since my youth," "people just like me." The cohesiveness of this class, both in term of personal relationships and shared outlook, was evident in their descriptions of themselves and others. They referred to "people who are congenial and from the same background," "people who share a common way of life and a common outlook," "people who are compatible." Mrs. Bennett, for example, spoke of her surprise when she learned in mid-life that there are people who feel left out of her social circle: "I'd never realized before that everybody didn't know everybody else."

Some of the women viewed themselves and others like them as decidedly better than others. They expressed a sense of moral, as well as social, superiority. Mrs. Brownley spoke of "nice people," and Mrs. Bennett, of "people of high principle." Mrs. Appleton (who had married into one of the city's oldest families and had, herself, attended an upper-class eastern boarding school) said that being upper class meant "morals, upbringing, not being permissive with your children . . . being productive and worthwhile." Mrs. Hall, as described in Chapter 1, had recently recognized her own "class snobbery" and was determined to rid herself of the moral superiority that she had been taught since childhood. This sense of superiority, as following chapters will show, was a recurring theme in the women's conversations with me.

Advantages

The most commonly cited advantage of being upper class was a topic otherwise hardly mentioned—the matter of great wealth and what it can buy. Some, like Mrs. Atherton, spoke of the opportunities available to her children: "We're able to send the children to any sort of school," she said. Others, like Mrs. Hughes, alluded to the material advantages: "I was born with a silver spoon in my mouth. I have all the worldly goods that anyone could want. I've never wanted for anything, and I've never envied anybody."

Mrs. Ames enjoys being surrounded by things of quality and beauty: "I was brought up in a home where I saw nothing but the best. It gives you a certain standard. You know what perfection is. I have lovely things, inherited from my family, and I know how to use them." Mrs. Appleton recognizes that other classes have more to worry about and spend more time doing the mundane tasks of daily life than people of wealth and privilege. She said: "My family was never hard up. We have more fun because we don't have to worry about things and spend time doing things like cleaning the stove." Several women mentioned that they didn't have to work for what they had. Mrs. Haines, for example, knows that she has "been very fortunate. If we want something, we get it, like a trip to Europe, without having to go and get a job."

The women felt that their lives were generally better than most people's, and some of their comments, again, had a tone of social and material superiority. With refreshing frankness, Mrs. Brownley acknowledged: "We're not supposed to have layers in society, but I suppose I do feel superior. I like people at my social level. They're awfully nice, and they're interested in doing and sharing what they've been blessed with—education, money, good food, travel, all those things some people don't have at all. They're interesting intellectually. I suppose there is in each of us that desire to rise to the top."

Mrs. Wilson felt her life was far easier than most people's lives:

"It's a very unpleasant world, and this is a little island of tranquility in an otherwise very unattractive world. It's easy to grow up like this. Everything is done for you. It's the way I'd like the whole world to be. It's pretty nice." She also implied that, although the life of her class is easier, people like herself deserve what they have. "I'd like the people who lead the community to have the kind of standards I have," she said. "I have high standards, personal, moral, educational, and cultural."

The women explicitly recognized that not being dependent on paid work made life better. Mrs. Farley pointed out that "there's a sense of well-being in not having to make an effort to achieve." Mrs. Nesbitt agreed, saying: "My life is like a storybook. It's a very unreal existence. I don't have to work and struggle. I have a successful husband and we're happy. I don't know how many happy people there are."

Thus, the women seemed fully cognizant of the privileges of their class. They spoke of wanting for nothing in material terms and of having generally happier and easier lives than most, and they talked of not having to make any effort to achieve what they have. Some women legitimated their inherited privilege by calling attention to the high moral standards and responsible leadership that they and their families had provided to the community. Other advantages derive from their family names and from their economic position, which present them with certain social opportunities.

The advantage of being accepted and respected in the community because of one's family was described by Mrs. Crowell, who said that "people are so friendly it's almost overwhelming. They know my father, and they know who we are. We didn't have to work to be accepted." Mrs. Smythe said: "I know my life would be very different if I had not lived in a city where I was born and raised and my family was known." Mrs. Vincent agreed, saying, "If we were new in the city we'd have to make ourselves known, which we've never had to do." Mrs. Wilson also thought this factor made her life more pleasant. "There are advantages to staying in the same community as I have," she said. "You stay where you know people and it makes life easier."

Being accepted by others also means having a sense of pride about yourself and your family. When asked about advantages of her position, Mrs. Ames called attention to this fact: "I'm very proud of what my family did. They were an integral part of the city." Women of the upper class understand that a well-known family name greases the wheels of social intercourse.

Being known also provides opportunities to influence community decision-making. Mrs. Howe, an astute, savvy woman who was chairperson of the city's Junior League, stated: "The definite advantage is that you have immediate access to people in decision-making capacities. They're not more than a phone call away." Mrs. Atherton said simply, "The door opens for position."

Mrs. Vincent spoke of the advantages of her position opening doors to employment and educational opportunities for her children. "My oldest daughter went for a job [at the company where her father is an officer]. She walked into the employment office of this huge corporation thinking the girl in the office couldn't possibly know who she was, and of course the girl picked it up right away and asked if her father wasn't an officer here. My daughter said yes, and the girl told her she'd better go through him. My youngest son walks through the door of his school everyday and sees his grandfather's name on the wall."

Disadvantages
There are certain disadvantages to the social position of upper-class women. Some women spoke of being too protected, and of never having a chance to prove themselves or to make their own way. Mrs. Haines—for whom the primary advantage of upper-class life was being able to get anything she wanted, being able to pay for a

trip to Europe without having to get a job—said of the negative side: "It's getting too much too soon. What are you going to do with the rest of your life if you have everything when you're born?" And Mrs. Ames regretted the lack of any opportunity to prove herself: "Perhaps the most difficult thing I had to deal with was whether I could have made it if I hadn't had anything."

Mrs. Carnes spoke of three of her friends who were currently getting divorces, suggesting that the issues cited by Mrs. Haines and Mrs. Ames were part of the problem: "I think the problem was they had too much money. They didn't have to make a commitment to anything. The husbands didn't have to work, and they moved around. Everything came too easily and they never had to fight for anything together."

This sort of comment previewed the most frequent response to the question: What one thing would you change if you had your life, thus far, to live over again? In response to this question (which is dealt with further in chapter 6) most of the women wished that they had worked before getting married, supported themselves and learned to stand on their own feet or, at least, prepared themselves to do so. At least some of the women felt that a disadvantage of being born to privilege is not having the opportunity to see what they could have accomplished through their own abilities.

Another disadvantage is the social expectation that everything always "go perfectly" in the upper-class family. Mrs. Wainwright (whose son's inheritance was cut off by his grandfather, the family patriarch, for "unacceptable behavior") spoke of her family problems: "You are never to talk about what is wrong in your life, only what was right. You live with the fear that family problems will come out. When I was a young bride and a young mother, the pressure to have things going perfectly was agonizing. My world collapsed very soon when my first-born needed psychiatric help. I was different in that I talked about my problems, and then some of the others would too. I know a family who have a child who is physically abnormal. He is now institutionalized. The father is a doctor, but it's been handled with great secrecy. Things are supposed to go well in the successful family. Children must be healthy in every respect, and also big. There is terrible competition about the age they do things."

Mrs. Hall told of her father's efforts to hide his problems from the family during the stock market crash of 1929: "My father went through the horrible crash and we were not allowed to talk about it. He would be called to the phone during dinner, and there was great concern that his dinner would be cold, when the call might be to tell him that so-and-so had committed suicide because he'd lost his fortune. Now it seems impossible, but that was the way mother and daddy wanted it. I felt terribly sheltered."

Mrs. Atherton, a "newcomer" had to travel frequently during the early days of her husband's career. She was unusually open about what this had meant for her own physical and mental health and that of their young children. When I suggested that it must be very difficult to deny or hide such problems, she said: "I have really heard very little adverse conversation about this among the people that I know, and yet I'm sure I'm not alone in my feelings. I guess they just live with it, or else they seek professional help—though it's still a dirty word if you're in psychotherapy. We in this socio-economic bracket are supposed to be better able to handle our problems than those further down the scale, and I don't think this is true at all. It seems to be assumed that since we've managed everything else so well, why not manage emotional problems too?"

pressure from one's class

Mrs. Atherton went on to imply that women of her class do not share personal and family troubles because it is bad for their husbands' business: "I think I would be a little reluctant to reveal any of [my own problems] to my peers for fear . . . it is a fear . . . that they would go to their husbands and tell them, and then their husband's feeling toward my husband would change. You have to present yourselves as a couple, as a united front. I wanted people to see me and my husband as an ideal couple."

Being known and having material privileges far beyond those

of other classes—privileges admittedly not earned by ones own effrots—can also incur resentment from others. Several of the women talked about this disadvantage of their class. Mrs. Ames who said that the main advantage of being upper class is having nothing but the best—said that a major disadvantage is that: "There is discrimination against the very wealthy. I try to keep my background a secret with some people, because there is immediate animosity. They say, 'You come from the lap of luxury. How could you know?' " Mrs. Carpenter had had similar experiences. "We're looked upon by the have-nots with a great deal of fear or hate," she said. "I've seen hate in people's faces." A somewhat softer version of this was expressed by Mrs. Nesbitt, who said, "I'm sure there are people who are envious of me."

Mrs. Wainwright, a self-proclaimed political radical and class rebel, was most explicit about the threat to her class. "When you're at the top, you're afraid of slipping," she said. "That's the terror of the upper class." She was equally explicit about the response of her class to any serious challenge to its position (her graduate training in social science evident in her analysis): "There's no conspiracy [to maintain position]. There doesn't need to be. There are patterns. The elite will be flexible as long as they can be. When they're threatened, they'll be violent, and they don't mean to lose."

At least some of the women are concerned, then, about class hostility and the potential for class conflict. Knowing that other classes resent upper-class privileges and position, they seek to legitimate their class privilege by fulfilling financial and volunteer obligations to the community, as will be discussed in Chapter 6. These sometimes burdensome obligations are cited as another disadvantage of upper-class position.

Recall Mrs. Sharpe, who greeted me by saying, "I suppose you'd like me to tell you about all the things my family has done for the city." When asked about the disadvantages of her way of life, she said: "It's the responsibility of living up to a name. You have a lot of giving to do. My husband and I spend night after night deciding how much money I should give to this or that. It is a lot of responsibility." Mrs. Brownley, who had frankly said that "it's nice to be part of the upper crust," made a similar comment: "It was a real challenge to see if I could do as well on community boards as my husband's family had done."

Mrs. Miles spoke of the push to do things she didn't want to do, as did Mrs. Howe, the community activist for whom the primary advantage of her position is having immediate access to the people who make the decisions. Mrs. Howe said: "If your family has been very active in the community, people have high expectations of you which you may or may not choose to meet. I was deluged when I came back home from college. It was just assumed I would be active. It's hard to say no to your parents' friends."

Mrs. Cooper (whose husband heads a well-known, national firm inherited from her father) said: "My dad gave so much to the community. It's a hard thing to live up to. I feel very responsible." While Mrs. Cooper felt she had father's high standards to live up to, Mrs. Langdon spoke of her mother as the reference point: "When you come from a family that has contributed so much, you feel pressured to accomplish yourself. You set goals and try to achieve as much. I wanted to show my mother that I could be my own person in the community. I think I've done that, but more is expected of you."

Some women apparently had had enough demands made on them for social responsibility and had decided to rest on their laurels. Several women told me, for example, that Mrs. Appleton was not very serious about her volunteer work, that all she did was serve now and then on club membership committees. Mrs. Appleton, who had said that "having more fun" is an advantage of her position, complained that "everyone expects you to donate to everything." Mrs. Nesbitt, who spoke earlier of her "storybook life," said of the disadvantages: "Everybody's after me to raise money. I've hated it all my life, and I don't do it anymore."

In spite of their complaints, these women know that they justify their inherited wealth and position by contributing in expected ways to the community. Although they eventually ease up on their contributions, all of the women I spoke with meet these expectations to some degree. They give what seems to them to be large sums of money to various institutions and groups, and they assume what they feel to be burdensome positions on the boards of community organizations. They appear to believe, to some degree, in the need to conform to the work ethic and the values of achievement that apply to the rest of American society—or risk challenges to their inherited position.

Summary and Conclusions

What does "upper class" mean to the women who were interviewed for this study? These women rarely used the more common measures of class position—achieved standards of income, occupation, or education—as criteria for class membership. Contrary to the more common mode of establishing the class position of women, they did not define their class position in relation to that of their husbands. Instead, they defined the meaning of class most often in terms of their own family ancestry and ascribed, as opposed to achieved, criteria.

Being from an old family is of primary importance to both the majority of the sample who were from such families and to those few who were not. While meeting the objective criteria for upper-class membership, and acknowledging that they are largely accepted into upper-class social circles, those few women not born into the oldest families still refer to themselves as "newcomers." They also believe that they will never be fully assimilated into the most established segment of the class. In addition to the historical matter of "birthright" (my term, not that of my subjects), the women spoke frequently about being "at the top" of the social hierarchy.

The women's descriptions of the meanings of class seem to support the view that class does in fact provide an organizational framework for their lives. This framework enables them to describe and explain their individual daily lives—their friendships with people of the same class, their standards of morality and propriety, and the pleasures and burdens of privilege. These desicriptions thus seem to challenge the more common belief that class frameworks are of little importance to people in the United States in organizing their daily lives.

The women's comments also begin to weave a picture of the upper-class way of life. Certain highlights begin to emerge. First, there is a clear preference for being with people like themselves, people they consider to be class equals and with whom they feel comfortable. There is also a general sense of being better than other people. This is not just a historical sense of having been here first or a social sense of occupying positions at the top of the social hierarchy; it is a moral sense. The women interviewed spoke of being more responsible parents, of being productive and worthwhile people who contribute to the community, and of being generally superior in moral terms. They are especially cognizant of their material privilege and of the fact that their lives are consequently easier and more pleasant than others people's lives. They also realize that they have exerted very little effort to acquire such privilege. Their social status and material resources enable them to form exclusive social and political circles and to have access to persons in positions of power. These exclusive circles and powerful positions, themselves, define the upper class.

Social status and material resources also lead to certain perceived limitations, pressures, and obligations—factors cited as the disadvantages of being upper class. The women interviewed feel

35

that others define and judge them primarily by who they are rather than by what they do. They feel that they will never know what they might have accomplished on their own. Since they are looked up to by others and pressured by class peers to uphold high class standards of family and personal life, they feel the need to maintain a public face to hide any private troubles. They also feel obligated to make significant contributions to their community and its major institutions in order to carry on the tradition of leadership established by their forefathers and foremothers.

Though community obligations are sometimes burdensome, the women seem to feel that contributing to the community is their primary way to justify their class privileges. They also imply the need to legitimate these privileges, lest their class position be challenged by others who might resent them. Thus what causes tensions in upper-class life is also sometimes seen as essential for maintaining that way of life. This contradiction is evident in the following chapter on the upper-class woman as wife.

Wife

3

"He expects me to make a nice home to come to, to be a cheery companion, to be ready to go on vacations when he wants to. He expects me to go along with what he wants to do."

"My husband has never helped around the house or done anything for the children. If I were starting life over he certainly would."

"He wanted to move to the country, and I didn't so we moved to the country."

"My husband never asks me what I think. He just tells me how its going to be."

They could be traditional wives anywhere. They could be sitting in working class bungalows, cramped city apartments, or suburban tract houses. But they aren't. The first woman, Mrs. Smythe, is described in Chapter 1. She arrived late for our interview, coming from a luncheon for the Friends of the Metropolitan Opera Association held at a nearby estate. Her uniformed maid ushered me to a sunroom to await her arrival. Mrs. Smythe's family is old enough and wealthy enough to have the library of an established local university named after them.

The next woman (who complained that her husband never helped around the house) is Mrs. Holt. A well-known and influential woman in the community, she is respected for her service on the boards of many of the city's health and educational institutions. Since she recently lost her full-time help, she rises at six each morning to make her husband's breakfast. She thinks that he could "help" by making his own breakfast. Our interview took place in the living room of her urban apartment, which occupies the entire floor of a building—a building whose extensive security system I had penetrated only because my appointment was known to the gatekeeper.

Mrs. Carpenter (the woman who had recently moved to the country) spoke with me in the plush blue and gold surroundings of her intown woman's club. The club's membership is invitational and limited to the oldest and wealthiest families in the city. She is the retiring president of the club. Mrs. Cooper, (the woman whose husband never asked her what she thought) was speaking specifically about decisions having to do with the company of which he is the president. The company is owned by her family, not his, and carries her family name—a name known to virtually every family in America.

In the previous chapter, much of what these women described as the meaning of upper class focused on the basic differences of their lives and the lives of other people. But as they talked about themselves as wives, their descriptions were strikingly similar to those of women in other classes. How do they see their responsibilities as wives? What are their expectations of themselves in that role?

Expectations

The upper class women I spoke with centered their lives around their husbands and their husbands' work and adapted themselves to the men's needs, performing what Jessie Bernard has called the "stroking" function. The stroking function, according to Bernard, consists of showing solidarity, giving help, rewarding, agreeing, understanding and passively accepting.

Mrs. Haines, for example, a young wife who mentioned as an aside toward the end of the interview that her husband was regularly out of town from Monday through Friday on business, remarked: "You have to be your husband's biggest booster. You have to make him feel good. He does not appreciate it if he comes home and I'm exhausted. I've got to be ready to find out what his week was like. He comes first, and I have to bend my life to fit his."

Mrs. Lane is an extremely protective wife in her fifties. Her husband heads one of the city's oldest and most prestigious shipping firms: "He's the brain in the family and it's my role to see that he's at his best. I've subjugated everything to that. When he comes home in the evening, this house must be perfectly quiet. I've told everyone the phone must not ring after five o'clock. He wants me to be pleasant, pretty and relaxed. I can't dare cry in front of him or show any emotion. I never bring a problem to him, except during forty-five minutes set aside on Sunday mornings for that purpose. I keep a list." When asked about her husband's responsibilities to her, Mrs. Lane conveyed the sense that the question had never occurred to her. "Oh, I think he's perfect," she said. "He's kind and considerate."

Mrs. Langdon (who offered that she had once called her

husband a male chauvinist for not appreciating her responsibilities at home) spoke of how important it was for her to be appreciative of him: "I have to be supportive. When he comes home, I have to be up no matter how I might feel or what kind of day I've had. I can tell the minute he walks in the door what kind of day he's had and what he needs. He doesn't know what kind of day I've had because I don't give him the chance." Similarly, Mrs. Wilson said that she helps her husband "with his ego problems by showing that I believe in him and his judgment."

Mrs. Atherton (the "newcomer" who spoke in the previous chapter of how personal and family troubles were bad for business) emphasized a protective role: "It's little things I do . . . like taking the telephone off the hook when he's home. He's so tired and he needs to relax. If he wants a sweater, I think I'm better equipped to go upstairs and get it. I used to try to protect him too much. There was never any dissention or anger in this house. I make life as comfortable as possible for my husband." She was the only woman who spoke of the sexual aspect of her responsibilities as wife, noting "sexual compatibility" as a part of making life comfortable for her husband. She added the importance of her looking attractive, saying, "When we go out, I like to know I will look as good as I can."

Mrs. Clarke (the wife of the young corporate lawyer who had just been made a partner in his family's old firm) made a comment similar to Mrs. Atherton's: "I keep myself in good order so I can be a responsive, loving and understanding wife when everything is going wrong." When I asked her to whom she turns when everything is going wrong for her, she, like Mrs. Lane, looked surprised and said: "I don't really have anyone to go to. I wish I did. I guess I'd go to my husband."

Mrs. Sharpe spoke of the importance of just being there, being attentive, as part of her stroking role. She said, "I try not to go to meetings in the evening and leave him alone." Mrs. Wilson also noted the importance of simply being available to her husband: "I'm here when he wants to blow up, when he wants me to listen."

Women of wealth and privilege, like women of other social classes, are expected as wives to accommodate to their husbands' emotional and other needs. Upper-class wives speak of their responsibilities to make their husbands feel good, to protect them from personal and family problems, to make life comfortable for them, to be loving and attractive partners, and simply to be available in case the men want something. They also speak of subjugating their own needs to those of their husbands. This mode of accommodation is the primary way in which upper-class women are clearly subordinate to their husbands. This mode runs throughout the other expectations of themselves as wives.

The women I spoke with take it for granted that they are solely responsible for "running the house." Though this expression does not mean doing the actual housework, which is the primary responsibility of women from other classes. Upper-class women are fully responsible, indeed perhaps more so, than wives of other classes for making sure that there is food on the table; clean and pressed clothes in the closets and dresser drawers of the various members of the family; and that the house is generally pleasant, clean, and in good order at all times. And, like other women, they do some complaining about that. The difference is that women of the upper class are far less responsible for actually cooking the meals, washing the laundry, and running the vacuum cleaner.

All of the women I spoke with have some kind of household help, although the extent of help varies and live-in help is by no means typical. Thus "running the house," for upper-class women, could be seen in the context of a statement made by Mrs. Holt. When asked how she and her husband divide up household responsibilities, she said "When you have someone else to do the work, there's not much dividing up to do." And Mrs. Atherton said of herself and other women of her social group: "Very few of us are doing mundane household chores. If I chose, I wouldn't have to lift a finger around the house. I like to cook when I have the time, but I think I enjoy it because I know I don't have to do it."

Upper-class women are not personally responsible for performing housework. They make decisions about how others, whose labor is purchased, perform the housework. For example, Mrs. Wilson spoke of planning, not cooking, meals; of ordering, not actually buying, foods. It is certainly the case, however, that the level of expectation in terms of what is done and how it is done is much higher.

Mrs. Clarke, for example, a rather harried young mother of three spoke poignantly of her husband and his long hours away from home, saying: "He wants a certain quality in his life. He likes the house well taken care of." Her earlier comment about her husband's time away from home reflects another expectation of wives who run the households for men who essentially run the nation's business. It is the expectation that the men will be absent much of the time. Mrs. Vincent (whose husband is an officer in a major national steel company) said, "He worked abroad for months. He expects there will be peace at home when he returns. I don't bother him with petty domestic details. He doesn't have time for that. His work is very demanding. I can't call and ask him what to do. He expects me to handle situations as they arise."

Mrs. Haines' husband is away five days a week; Mrs. Hammond's husband had been out of the country for the better part of five years setting up an overseas branch of the firm he now heads; and Mrs. Vincent's husband "worked abroad for months at a time." These women are examples of upper-class wives running their households in complete isolation from their husbands. Other studies have found this rigid division of responsibilities between husbands and wives in upper economic groups, though they have not noted the extent to which husbands are often absent. A study done by sociologists Blood and Wolfe twenty years ago concluded that "the more successful the husband is in his occupation, the less the wife can count on his help at home."[1] Helen Hacker concurs, saying "traditionally, the roles of husband and wife in the upper class are clearly separated."[2]

Most upper-class wives know that they can enhance their husbands' position by running the house and by protecting their husbands from domestic concerns. Since the women take care of the domestic front, the men are free to concentrate their energies on business and community activities. Mrs. Cooper put this particularly succinctly: "If a man's home life is happy, he can put his all into being a dynamo in the business world." When asked how she helps her husband with work, Mrs. Harper said: "I help just by not upsetting him and keeping the house running."

Mrs. Hammond added, "A leader in the business community has to know the home front is protected. That's just a woman's job." She was especially aware of the importance of her job at home in allowing her husband to reach the very top of the corporate structure: "He set up the international branch of (his firm). He was gone most of the time for five years. He didn't have to worry about the children or the house because he knew I was going to do it. I had my last child then—because I just didn't have anything else to do." When asked what she thought would have happened if she had objected to his being away during those five years, she responded without hesitation: "He probably wouldn't be the chairman of the board today."

Several other women said that they help their husbands' careers by simply doing whatever is necessary for their husbands to be happy and successful in work, and by adjusting their own lives to their husbands' desires. Mrs. Haines (the young wife whose husband was out of town five days out of every seven) said: "We've been married eight years and he's always traveled. Usually he's away Monday through Friday. I've adjusted to it. I've learned to fill my days. I feel he's a better husband when he's doing what he does.

43

I've learned to keep busy during the week, because when he comes home he doesn't want to go out much. I've molded my life to his."

Most of the women mentioned that they are also responsible for their families' "social arrangements," though only the newcomers spoke of an obligation to entertain in order to advance their husbands' position. Women from old established families seem to feel that the men can make it on their own merits and do not need this kind of help from their wives. Mrs. Haines feels she is "fortunate to be married to a man who says that if he can't make it on his own, my being able to whip up a Beef Wellington is not going to help him. He considers [entertaining] frosting on the cake."

Entertaining clients or prospective associates is, thus, not seen by upper-class couples as a way to climb the ladder of success. These are men and women born to privilege, and social striving is not necessary. It is assumed that the men will acquire the top positions due them in a matter of time. Business entertaining among the old upper class, therefore, is more a demonstration of having already attained the most powerful positions in the corporate hierarchy, rather than a means of achieving those positions—as might be the case with rising young executives from other socioeconomic classes.

Older women whose husbands had achieved the very top positions in the corporate world, confirmed this view. Mrs. Farley (who is married to a man who heads a firm founded by his family) said succinctly, "We don't do business entertaining. We're the ones who are entertained." These women did sometimes speak of an annual ritual, for which they were responsible, to entertain the husbands' employees. The views of the upper-class women from old families are essentially the reverse of the upper-middle-class and upward-striving executives' wives. That is, young women from old families whose husbands' careers are less well established, are not likely to see business entertaining as a way to advance their
 husbands' positions; while other women, whose husbands are at

the top of their firms, do seem to think that business entertaining is important—not as a way to advance their husbands' career, but rather as a way to express their gratitude to their husbands employees for jobs well done during the year. The story is different for newcomers to the upper class, as evidenced by a comment from Mrs. Atherton who "did have the obligation of entertaining clients. I wanted people to see us as an ideal couple and to see me as very efficient in entertaining. That's where a woman fits in to a husband's work. There isn't a partner hired in the firm now where they don't look over the qualities of the wife. If my husband were to consider a new partner for the firm, he would make it his business to be entertained in their home to look over the wife. When we entertain maybe 150 people for dinner at the club, it's mostly for business. Out of this number, maybe fifteen couples are really good friends, people we enjoy being with." For the newer upper-class families, then, entertaining is one of the ways to become accepted by the established upper class.

"Making social arrangements" is a broader social form than "entertaining." It is one of the ways that upper-class women construct and maintain the social fabric of upper-class life as discussed in the introduction to this study. The women see to it that the social network of "congenial" people is kept in good order. Mrs. Clarke, for example, said that her husband expects her to have "people around that he enjoys, to do things with." Mrs. Harper, a mother of five (whose husband is a partner in one of the city's oldest corporate law firms) said: "When he's worked hard all day and he calls up and says let's get a tennis game together, I do it. He'd get upset if I didn't. . . . If he wants me to organize a party, I have to get it done. If he calls me in the middle of the morning and wants to have a party the next day, I've got to do it."

Making social arrangements supports the exercise of power in the business world. Since the woman is responsible for arranging the man's social as well as home life, the man is free to concentrate all his energies on the nation's economic affairs. As Mrs. Hall concluded, "The wife takes care of social arrangements and leaves the husband to business."

Being available to travel with their husbands on business trips is the first of three expectations related directly to their husbands' work. The importance of this responsibility of upper-class wives was expressed by Mrs. Harper: "I have to be available and ready [to travel]. If he wants to go on a trip, I'd better be ready. My theory is that if I'm not available he'll find someone else who is."

Mrs. Cooper spoke of monthly trips she had been making with her husband: apparently most business travel includes specific activities for the wives, on the assumption that they will, of course, accompany their husbands. Mrs. Farley noted: "When we travel to meetings, my function is to attend the ladies' meetings, and in the evenings we get together with other couples. I don't mind it, but it's tiring. They program the wives as much as the men."

Business travel by upper-class couples enhances national class networks. The importance of such travel and the need for women to be available to go along are reflected in discussions of the advantages of volunteer work. (This issue is considered in Chapter 6.) Volunteer work they explained, provides them with the flexible schedules necessary to accompany their husbands on his business trips.

Another task of upper-class wives is to be a "sounding board" for their husbands' business concerns. The women spoke repeatedly and with resonating sameness of the importance of this role. They described explicitly how passive listening and acceptance, not active participation, was wanted of them. Mrs. Harper said bluntly, "I listen, and I keep my mouth shut." Similarly, Mrs. Vincent thought that her husband is "just looking for a sounding board, not real advice."

Though these kinds of comments were typical, a few of the

women did think they had at times given useful advice. Mrs. Sharpe spoke of her husbands' unhappiness in a former job: "I urged him to leave and to go to another company. He's much happier now."

Mrs. Carnes is an ambitious young wife who wants her upward-striving husband to follow in the footsteps of her father, the chairman of the board of a major international firm. She feels that she helps her husband achieve these goals: "He talks to me a lot about business. He thinks I can understand. I help him make decisions . . . about purchasing a company, changing jobs, giving a presentation. I hope he's going to the top. I think he's terrific. I don't know if it's helped him or hurt him, the connection with my father. He has to prove himself every step of the way. He adores my father, and I think he's a model for him. I'm ambitious, so it would be hard if he weren't. I'd like him to have his own company. He doesn't do well working for other people."

Some of the women also talked about their role in the socialization of younger executive wives—women married to the men who work for their husbands. Mrs. Lane (the extremely protective wife of the president of an old city firm) said: "Whenever a new executive wife comes along I give her quite a lecture on ceasing to be an emotional person. She should never be nervous or cross. These men can't take that. She should always be prompt and ready to go." Mrs. Lane has recently found that the younger wives were not as willing as they used to be: "I find the newer wives want to be people. They feel they have as many rights as their husbands. They say they could never do what I ask, that they're equals."

Socializing young wives did not always mean teaching them to conform to husbands' demands. Recognizing the difficulties caused by the frequent moving that is part of corporate life, two of the women—both newcomers—had opposed their own husbands on this issue. Mrs. Atherton, speaking of one young wife whose husband had been offered a promotion and a transfer in the firm headed by Mr. Atherton, said, "Large companies sometimes move their executives indiscriminately without much concern with what it's going to be like for the rest of the family. For big daddy, it's a step up the ladder. Some of the people in my husband's firm have had promotions offered and the man has turned them down because his wife objected. One I know had grown children and good friends here and a new home. She didn't want to leave. I was supportive to her in her decision. My husband would have felt it was none of my business, and he didn't know I was involved."

Mrs. Nesbitt also expressed concern about the effect of frequent moves and described how she had tried to be helpful to the wives: "I've talked to my husband about it, but he says sometimes he just has to [move his younger executives]. He realizes that it's hard on the women and it's important that the marriage be happy. He makes sure that the wife is going to be able to adjust. I've tried to get some of the wives [at my husband's company] into things in the community when I knew they were unhappy. Some told me they were unhappy, that they hated [the city]. I made an effort to see that they were invited to join things." These comments by Mrs. Atherton and Mrs. Nesbitt are important because they represent rare examples of upper-class women opposing upper-class men on an issue and siding with other women.

In regard to expectations of wives, then, these upper class women, describe a general mode of accommodation and a number of specific tasks. The general mode consists of adjusting, "molding," their own lives to the lives of their husbands—a mode that is inevitably one of subjugation. In terms of tasks, they are expected to run the house and shield their husbands from mundane household and family concerns. They free the men to concentrate all of their energies on their work, work that sometimes necessitates long absences from home. The women are also responsible for making the social arrangments that support the fabric of upper-class life.

Tasks directly related to their husbands' work are the need to travel with their husbands on business trips and to serve as sounding boards for their husbands' business concerns (only rarely giving real advice). The wives of men who head business firms may also be called upon, or take it upon themselves, to socialize the wives of new men hired into the firm. These tasks reflect a rigid division of labor between men and women of this class, which differs somewhat in content but not substantially in form from the division of men and women in other socioeconomic classes.

The wives' tasks reflect not only the division of labor, or social differentiation, but also a clear subordination of the women to the men, a social stratification based on gender. This is particularly true of the expectations that wives be accommodating, adaptive, available. This general mode makes it difficult, if not impossible, for the women to have life agenda independent of the men. This mode of subjugation seems inherent in all the tasks for which the women are responsible. They not only run the house, they do so in a way that shields their husbands from any concern over what goes on there; they do so even when he is away from home for extended periods of time. They not only make the social arrangements, they make them on short notice and at their husband's request. They not only travel with their husbands on business—a task that surely has its pleasant aspects—but they do so also on short notice, which means that their own schedules must be open and flexible. They not only are available to listen to their husbands talk about business problems, they also learn, for the most part, to hold their tongues and not give any real advice. This evidence of gender stratification, and subjugation of upper-class women calls attention to the need for a gender as well as a class conceptual framework for understanding these women's lives.

Decisions and Money
Gender as well as class stratification was evident as the women talked about family decision-making. Major decisions were described as changes in place of residence, childrens' schooling, hus-

bands' job, or the wife's decision to take paid employment or return to school. These decisions were made, most women said confidently, by themselves and their husbands together. Some of the women, however, qualified this. Mrs. Smythe, implying basic agreement with her husband on most issues, said:"If he thinks it's a good idea, it doesn't take too long for me to think so too. He can usually convince me he's right."

Mrs. Holt implied the use of feminine wiles: "I think the woman often has her way of getting what she wants. Some of her decision making may not seem so obvious. [My husband and I] have had our share of disagreements." Mrs. Lane claimed that since her and her husband's views were essentially the same, making decisions was an almost automatic joint venture: "I have a very brilliant husband, and I tend to have the same views as he does, to repeat what he says. But we make decisions together, and I think he respects my opinion."

Mrs. Crowell (the young wife who had complained to her husband about his frequent traveling, but had not noticed that it made any difference) said: "We talk things over. I made a lot of decisions because he's not here. He says he feels left out sometimes. Major decisions we make together—his new job, the new house, any change in the childrens' school, whether I would go to school."

Mrs. Garson, an elderly woman and a recent widow claimed that her husband need not have worked at all, that they could have lived on her family inheritance. She said of decisions: "I think I was more likely to bring up problems and issues and ask him what he thought. If he didn't like it, we probably didn't do it."

Although the women claimed almost universally that they made decisions "together" with their husbands, it appeared that, in fact, the husband had the decision-making power in the family. When important, recent decisions were analyzed, the power structure of the family was clearly gender stratified, with the men in a position of dominance: their wills prevailed in important decisions.

Mrs. Appleton's statement is indicative of this phenomenon. Her husband had just changed jobs, and she reported that they had made the decision "together." When I asked her what would have happened if she had actively opposed the job change (which she did not like because it was going to mean more entertaining of clients and less time spent with her husband), she laughed and said, "He probably would have said 'so what!' "

Mrs. Crowell, whose husband had recently been promoted, gave the "partnership" answer in response to my question of how decisions were made. She then went on to offer: "I don't think he would have refused [the promotion] even if I'd said I absolutely don't want you to take it. He came home a few weeks ago and told me he'd be doing more traveling even though he knew I wouldn't like it."

Such evidence suggests that upper-class women, like women of other social classes, have less equalitarian marriages in terms of family decision-making than they, themselves, believe. Lillian Breslow Rubin found this same false belief about equalitarian decision-making in her study of working-class couples. She reports that "most people said 'fifty-fifty.' Yet, when one pushes the question a little further the illusion is quickly dispelled. Almost all agree: the husband has veto power over a decision."[3]

I was interested in the fact that upper-class husbands dominate family decision-making. Studies of women and families in other classes have found that power over money is a primary factor in deciding how much of a voice the women have. Upper-class women have substantial inheritances independent of their husbands. How, therefore, are the husbands able to maintain their power? For an answer to this question, I began to look at the issue of money and its link to family power.

When asked about their own money and what it meant to them, the women readily acknowledged its effect on their lives. They spontaneously offered comments about the effect that having

51

their own money has on their relationships with husbands. Mrs. Bennett, an elderly widow, said: "I had my own money and made decisions about investing without consulting my husband. It was very important to me. It's hard to have to ask your husband for money."

Mrs. Hall, who had married down in class, said: "I have my own money. [My husband] insisted on paying the household bills. My money went for fripperies like horses. He set himself up a goal that he was going to earn as much money as I had. It's very important for me to have my own money." She went on to say that she had recently begun handling her own money: "I didn't used to do my own accounts. I was being very childlike. My husband's secretary did my accounts. After a while I didn't like that. I wanted to be able to buy things without its going through my husband's office. I didn't want everyone to know how much everything cost. So now I handle my own accounts, and I enjoy it immmensely."

Mrs. Haines (a young woman who had married into a family of old money) said: "Nobody can say I married my husband for his money because I can match him. I find that very comfortable because we're equals. So many of my friends are not, and if their husbands are tightwads they have to finagle it. I have my own money with which I buy whatever I need for myself. I pay for all the help and I pay for the food. My husband pays other bills and [the children's] education."

Mrs. Sharpe (a woman from one of the city's oldest and wealthiest first families) said: "The household money is mostly mine, partly his. My mother left me a large sum of money. I've been able to give gifts I otherwise couldn't have." She did not, however, make her own investment decisions: "I don't want to make investment decisions. I'd rather have my husband do that. He asked me about it."

Mrs. Holt (who noted that her husband never helped around the house) said that when she pays the household bills it is with his money. She said of the little money she has of her own: "I use my money for personal things. It's nice having a little of my own. I don't have to explain all my purchases and contributions."

Mrs. Brownley had married into one of the city's first families and was one of the few in the sample to openly acknowledge that she enjoyed her husband's financial status because it "made [her] life very pleasant." Of household finances, she said: "Paying for the children's clothing was up to me. Paying for their education was his responsibility. He pays for the electric bills, the plumbing, and the taxes. I pay for the groceries from a household allowance. I have a small amount of money of my own which I invest through a broker. It's nice to have something that's truly your own. You can buy gifts or do whatever you want with it."

Mrs. Cooper (whose husband heads a company bearing her family name) remarked: "I get a household allowance from my husband's bank account, though I can't say I don't have money of my own. It's in a savings account, and it goes for special things. Most of it is invested. My daughter is about to be married, and I know my husband had some financial problems recently, so it's nice not to have to go to him and say I need some extra in my allowance."

Mrs. Langdon had been able to use her own money as leverage for avoiding a task that her husband wanted her to do: "I have a small amount of money of my own. I can buy gifts for my husband or buy a piece of art work he might not like. He pays the bills. He said he thought it would be good if I did that, and I said I thought it would be good if he did the cooking [as a way of letting him know I did not want to pay the bills]."

Mrs. Garson the elderly widow who had said that she and her husband could have lived on her inheritance said: "I was glad to be able to give to the community as we have, and have an easy life. I guess our life would have been quite different if we'd have to live on his income."

Most of the women, as their comments indicate, fully enjoy having their own money and recognize the freedom and independence it gives them. A few, however, said that having their own money is of little importance to them. They claimed that, since their husbands do not use money as a source of power, having their own money doesn't make that much difference to them. Mrs. Martin who spoke of "doing her share" in raising the children and of "being a good companion" as her responsibility as a wife said of financial matters: "Since I don't have a tightwad for a husband, having money of my own hasn't made much difference to me. I don't really think about it."

Mrs. Hammond (whose husband had been out of the country for the better part of five years setting up an international branch of his firm) said that she pays "all the bills from a joint account. I could have inherited some money from my mother but I persuaded her to pass me for the children. I don't feel the need for money of my own for personal security. I never think about it."

Mrs. Farley (who had said she did not do business entertaining because she and her husband were the ones who were entertained) said of household finances: "We pool it all. I pay the bills. I don't have much money of my own. He has to approve what I buy. It doesn't bother me. I've been lucky because he's been very good about it."

Mrs. Nesbitt (a woman in her sixties who seemed to be especially happy in her marriage claiming that "marriage gets better like good wine") says of money matters at home: "I get an allowance, but I don't have to pay for anything with it. I spend it any way I want. [My husband] doesn't ask what I do with it. It was his idea, and I haven't had to ask for any increases. My husband's secretary pays the bills. My father left me some money, but it's in stocks and bonds. The bank manages them. It doesn't have any importance to me."

A direct link between money and family decision-making

was made by Mrs. VanHague, the only woman who professed to be the major decision-maker in her marriage. This elderly dowager, now a widow, responded to my question about major money decisons, saying: "I made most of the decisions because he figured it was my money."

The relationship of economic power to financial decision-making is also evident in the cases of three women with whom I was able to trace actual, recent decisions. The husbands of women who do not control their own money appear to have the major share of the power. Mrs. Appleton (who laughingly said that her husband would have paid little attention to her objections to his new job) reported that, although she does have some money of her own, she sees her husband in the traditional role of "provider": he pays all of the household bills, and she appears to know little of financial matters. Mrs. Crowell (who said that she did not think her husband would have turned down his promotion even if she had absolutely opposed it, and who is contemplating enrolling in graduate school in special education) indicated that, although she has some money of her own, she "would like to be more independent. It's part of the reason why I want to work."

Mrs. Carpenter and her husband had recently moved to a large country estate. When I asked her how they had decided on the move, she answered without cracking a smile: "He wanted to move to the country, and I didn't. So we moved to the country." Later in the interveiw she said of household finances: "He gives me a household allowance. If I need more usually it's quite a scene. I send him to the store so he knows how much things cost. Then he comes home and says he sees what I mean about the prices. Or sometimes I'll be cagey about it and give him hot dogs or hamburgers until he asks how much of a raise I want."

Mrs. Appleton had said earlier that she objects to her husband's travel and late hours, but that "he doesn't listen to me, so there isn't much point of making an issue of it." She had also said that the most important thing was for her husband to be happy, and that it "didn't really matter" what she thought. When asked about household financial arrangements, she said: "He gives me a monthly allowance and then we hassle over the rest of it. If I needed more and he was in a generous mood, he just might give it to me. If he wasn't, he'd say, 'What's it for this time? ' or 'I think you've had enough.' " As to her own family money, Mrs. Appleton said: "I've turned it over to my husband to invest."

In sum, it appears that having control over their own money is as important for upper-class wives as it is for wives in other social classes. This is especially true when it comes to having a say in family decisions. Whether the husband is a cab driver, a clerk, or a chairman of the board, the women's voices are heard more loudly in homes where they are economically independent. In households where having money of her own makes little difference, the wife sees her husband as an exceptional man—a man who recognizes his wife's contribution to the family in her own right, provides her with an allowance comparable to a "salary," and does not ask questions about how she spends it. When wives are expected to justify their expenditures and to make elaborate appeals for increases, the scenes in the upper-class households are very much the same as those in any other household. This was evident from the women's descriptions of "finagling it," like Mrs. Carpenter who sent the husband to the grocery store, or serving him budget meats for several days in a row.

It is difficult for wives to have to ask their husbands for money; and women who have to do so are inevitably in a position of subordinance. If the husband checks up on how his wife spends the money he gives her, it is cause for resentment on both sides. Even when he is "good about it," the women are aware that they are "lucky"—a word that implies the lack of control on the woman's part and the recognition that, if he were not "good about it," there wouldn't be much she could do.

At least some of the women are displeased about their lack of an equal voice in family decisions and see a link between this and their financial control. I then wondered how the women's control or lack of control over their own money relates to the division of household labor. I found that the women who are economically self-reliant, due to an inheritance or a salary, seem to have different ideas about family and household responsibilities than the women who rely economically on their husbands. Women who manage their own money had less traditional views about their roles as wives.

Mrs. Hoight, whose husband's expectations for her are rigid, described with some guilt her unwillingness to go along with his wishes: "He'd like it if I stayed home more than I do and was more supportive. I should devote myself to being interested in the things he is. I do feel a lot of guilt about my housekeeping. My husband says he would like more order, more meals on time. It could become a major conflict, but it never has." When I asked her how she and her husband manage money, she replied: "I have a small income from my father-in-law. The money I have is my own to manage. I buy and sell my own stocks. I make my own decisions about investments."

Mrs. Ames also expressed nontraditional views about her responsibilities as a wife. She sees it as her role to "bring love and joy, to do my part on the team. I've always been a liberated woman, as independent as I wanted to be." Like Mrs. Hoight, she has money of her own that she uses to her advantage: "I pay the bills, often out of my own money. The women I know who married a husband with no money of their own are far more subservient than I've been. I mentioned it to one of my friends once and she said, 'Don't forget he's buying everything I have. I wouldn't have anything if it weren't for him, so I have to do it his way.' Those women are in a completely different situation from mine."

Mrs. Spears (the only woman who had had a full-time, paid

professional career for some years) described her relationship with her husband as follows: "[My husband and I] have a partnership. We don't have distinct roles. I think that's because I've always worked."

Mrs. Martin (the only woman who indicated that she and her husband discussed, rather than assumed the division of labor at home) said: "I do the inside and he does the outside [of the house]. We've had to decide who performs which functions." When asked initially how she saw her responsibilities as wife, she used the phrase "do my share," saying: "I am to run the house, be happy, make a pleasant atmosphere, do my share in raising the children, be a good companion in his interests." Like the other women who strayed from the most traditional role expectations, Mrs. Martin is financially self-sufficient. When I asked how she and her husband dealt with money matters, she answered: "I am very fortunate in having some money of my own, so I've had an independence."

Mrs. Howe was the only woman who indicated that she had made some real changes in how tasks got done at home. In regard to finances, she said: "I am fortunate to have a supplementary income, and if I didn't, I would really miss it. It gives me a definite independence."

Mrs. Carnes (who has recently taken a part-time job, has a full-time live-in "girl," and ambitions that her husband will follow in her father's highly successful footsteps) said that her responsibilities as a wife were "to be supportive, to be my husband's best friend. I don't hold back if there are problems at home," she said, "lots of wives buffer their husbands from that. I don't believe in that, though I suppose he'd like me to be more of a homebody." When asked about division of work at home, Mrs. Carnes declared: "My husband is totally involved in the care of the [children]. He gives bottles, bathes, changes diapers. He's the best father I know." When asked about household finances, Mrs. Carnes, too, focused on the importance of her own money: "My husband had no money at all when we were married, and we could never have this lifestyle if it weren't for my money."

In contrast to these women who manage their own money are the women who speak of their husbands' lack of involvement at home. Mrs. Holt (the older woman with grown children who said that if she had things to do over, her husband would contribute much more to home and children) said of household finances: "I pay the bills, but it's his money."

Mrs. Lane is a stirring and extreme illustration of how a wife's financial dependence affects her behavior. She is the executive wife so protective of her husband that the phone dare not ring after five o'clock, and so intimidated by him that she only dares to discuss problems during the weekly forty-five minutes set aside for that purpose. At the end of the interview, when asked how she would categorize her family's social position, Mrs. Lane described her own financial position before her marriage: "My family lost everything in the crash of '29. But it's all worked out, because I married well."

Virtually all of the women I spoke with—unlike Mrs. Lane—had inherited their money from their own families. But the issues of money, power, and division of labor are not simply related to *having* their own money (which is taken for granted among these women) but rather to controlling and managing it. Like Mrs. Appleton and Mrs. Sharpe, most of the women had given up control of their inheritances, turning them over to their husbands to manage. This appears to be a largely unquestioned gender expectation of upper-class women—though a few, like Mrs. Hall and Mrs. Bennett, had questioned it.

Why are these women—who have the economic base to exert greater power in families than women more objectively economically dependent on husbands—so subordinate to the men of their class? Searching my data for evidence of their own recognition of their subordinate position, I looked first at the dissatisfaction the women had regarding their home and family responsibilities.

Dissatisfactions

I did not ask the women directly about their satisfaction or dissatisfaction with their role as wives. What they chose to tell me, therefore, was unsolicited and in the context of other questions. Not suprisingly, it was often emotionally charged as well. Their husbands' frequent traveling was a matter of particular displeasure, especially when there were small children to consider.

Mrs. Wilson, who was born into an old family and married somewhat down in class, said when I asked her how she had helped her husband in his work: "He's a compulsive worker. Once he went out of town four days a week, for a year. I was home with three kids, and it was pure hell. Nobody to talk to. I just had to hang in there. I don't think men realize how much women contribute to the family." When asked how she and her husband divided up responsibilities at home, she said: "Being a wife carries much the same responsibilities as being a mother. My husband's just one of the children. He doesn't have a lot of responsibility around the house. The next generation isn't going to accept that. Men are living in a fool's paradise. I never have time to really think, and I don't think I've ever talked to anyone as I have to you [in this interview]. I'm always running up and down. A woman's time is cut into little tiny segments. I really do resent it. Women don't have many choices."

Recall Mrs. Holt's comments at the beginning of this chapter: "My husband has never helped around the house or done anything for the children. If I were starting life over he certainly would. I encourage him now to help with the housework more than I ever have before."

Mrs. Howe, a young wife with school-age children answered my question about how she had helped her husband's career by saying: "He's worked every Saturday for as long as I can remember. I don't like it, and he knows I don't like it. I feel it places tremendous strain on the family. He also has to travel a lot and work evenings. A few years ago he was always late for dinner, and I finally put my foot down and said you can't keep a family together without sharing time."

Mrs. Crowell is another young wife, who is seriously considering a career of her own. Of her husband (who is going to school part-time in addition to his job in an old established firm in the city) she said: "He's not home much now that he's in school, but it's not so bad now that the children are older. I used to just hate the dinner hour when the children were younger and he had to be out of town . . . I accept [the travel] grudgingly. I don't like it but it's just the way things are. I've let my thoughts be known, but I don't think it's ever made any difference. He goes anyway, but we talk it over."

Mrs. Clarke spoke of her husband's traveling and long working hours: "When I don't see him for great long times, I get very annoyed. After we get back together, we're annoyed with each other instead of just being happy to be together."

Mrs. Atherton, whose children were grown, responded to the question of how she and her husband divided up responsibilities: "He traveled a great deal [when the children were younger], so I was put in the role of both mother and father. I was angry and resentful."

In a variation on this theme, Mrs. Hall objected to her husband's expectations that she travel *with* him on business. She recognized that his demands affected whatever efforts she might make to have an independent life or serious work of her own: "If I started traveling with him, then whatever I would be involved in would be for nothing. If you travel all the time with your husband, then you've got to cancel your own appointments. That says that your appointments aren't important, that your work doesn't mean anything."

Like Mrs. Hall, several of the women expressed dissatisfac-

61

tion that their work outside the home is not respected or supported by husbands. This is true of both volunteer work and paid work, a matter to be considered further in Chapter 6. Many of the women reported that husbands fear their taking paid jobs, which is seen as a reflection of the men's inability to provide financially. At this economic level, such a phenomenon is surprising. It speaks to the power of traditional gender roles—in this case, man as provider—even when the economic class renders such roles unnecessary.

Mrs. Carpenter's husband, for example, was particularly negative about her chairing several local boards: "It would have been an affront to my husband for me to get a job, a sign that he couldn't support me in the manner to which I was accustomed. I was furious at first, but if you love somebody you don't defy them, so I just sulked." At the same time, she has refused to lessen her extensive volunteer activities, saying with icy calm: "If he doesn't like it, he can go to hell. Marriage is a compromise, and that's something he can compromise on."

Similarly, Mrs. Bennett said that she had wanted to have a job after she was married, but did not do so because: "My husband didn't take to it. He thought it would look as though he couldn't support me, so I didn't want to hurt his feelings."

Some women said that their husbands objected to their working outside the home because it would mean that they would be less available or would interfere with their husbands' own work schedules or other interests. Mrs. Carnes, who had recently taken a part-time paid job, said of her husband: "He does notice that I'm preoccupied sometimes, and he doesn't like that. He'd like me to be a homebody, but he's given up on that long ago. He knows it's not for me, and he's generally supportive."

Mrs. Langdon's husband had posed economic as well as social reasons for opposing his wife's thoughts of paid work: "[My husband] has said that my taking a job would mean that we would have to give up a lot of the things I would like to do, and as long as we don't need the money he thinks it's foolish. He feels I'm being more personally rewarded for [the volunteer work] I'm doing. He would probably also figure out what it would mean for him in taxes."

Mrs. Harper, whose husband was very supportive of her volunteer work, described his attitude toward her taking a paid job: "I think he'd like it fine as long as it didn't interfere with his schedule."

Mrs. Vincent, a woman who was particularly unresolved about her work situation, reported: "I've never had a paid job. I have suggested several times recently to my husband that I go back to school and get a master's degree or get a regular job. He's not a bit enthusiastic about that. About a year ago, I realized he was quite earnest about it, so of course I haven't pursued it. I think there would be great satisfaction in having a regular job."

Mrs. Hoight (who claimed that her husband was so negative about her involvement in volunteer activities that he refused to attend the meetings she conducted) said of his attitude toward paid work for her: "I think if it were a job where I could take some extra time off it would be okay, but if we ran into a situation where he wanted to go away and I couldn't, he'd be very distressed. He says my taking a job is a dumb idea."

The very few women who had paid jobs or were in school full-time at the time of the interview all reported that their husbands were supportive. For example, Mrs. Spears (who claimed that she and her husband had a "partnership" rather than "distinct roles") is a full-time academic. Nonetheless, she offered: "Still, I do feel the overall running of the house is my responsibility." She also described her frustration at having her own accomplishments ignored: "Almost nobody knows what I do. Sometimes it makes me angry. I still go places where they introduce everybody at the speaker's table, and I'm there because of my husband, and they don't even bother to find out if I do something besides be his wife. They could at least ask."

Mrs. Crowell, a mother seriously contemplating a return to

professional school, said of her husband: "I think he'd think it was great. He's pushed me." When asked if she thought her going to school would change her husband's role at home she said: "I suppose it would. We haven't really discussed that. I just think he'd do it. I suppose the day to day work is mine. I may get paid help."

It appears, then, that upper-class wives share with their counterparts in other social classes husbands who may object to their work involvements outside the home, whether in unpaid community activities, paid jobs, or schooling. Some studies of this issue report that ". . . the public's attitude toward working wives [has] gone from the unacceptable exception to the approved norm."[4] A recent study claims that seventy-five percent of husbands now support the right of married women to be employed.[5] Rubin, however, presents evidence (1976) of negative attitudes of working-class husbands toward their wives working outside the home;[6] and studies continue to report that wives take major responsibility for their households even when working outside.[7] The upper-class women I spoke with are well aware of this. They know that they need the support of their husbands to make changes in their work lives; and when they contemplate such changes, they seem to expect that they will continue to be responsible for runing the house—or making the decisions about its running. They also seem to expect that their husbands will not make any major adjustments in their own lives. This is a source of dissatisfaction among upper-class women, just as it is among women of other classes.

Studies by Jessie Bernard and Anne Locksley, among others, have shown that wives are generally less satisfied and more frustrated with their marital relationships than their husbands.[8] And upper-class women, like women of other socioeconomic levels, have not been very successful in changing the gender-based divisions of tasks at home. Only one of the women I spoke with, Mrs. Howe, had actually been able to change the way she and her husband handle home responsibilities. A dynamic young community leader, who describes herself as an "equaliterian," she spoke with assurance and style: "How we divide things up has changed a lot over the past few years. I used to feel it was all my responsibility. Now we all pitch in and do our share. I taught [the children] to do it, and gradually my husband just picked it up. We did talk about equalizing roles in the family, because it was important to me that [the children] grow up with this."

Mrs. Howe is decidedly the exception to the rule among upper-class women. Even in this most priviledged class—among women who have substantial money of their own, who can hire other women to do the everyday, nitty-gritty housework, and who are their husbands' class equals—gender stratification is clearly evident, and change is minimal. Why?

One source of subordinance among upper-class women—as a general mode of accomodation and in family decision-making—is the class tradition of women turning over their inheritances to their husbands to manage. When the women give up the control of their money, they give up the freedom to order their own lives and the ability to speak with an equal voice in family decisions. This is not surprising. Low economic power has long been shown to be related to low decision-making power in families in other social classes.[9] Why, then, do upper-class women give up control of their money? The interviews indicate that they know the control of their own money is related to their position relative to husbands. The simplest answer, therefore, is probably subscription to traditional gender roles and traditional gender role socialization. In our culture, the male role dictates that men be the primary economic providers and decision-makers: it is primarily their job to earn and control the money. Upper-class women, by turning their inheritances over to their husbands, are simply adhering to this general expectation within their class.

Traditional gender role expectations do not, however, tell the whole story. There is a more unique class explanation for this common practice of upper-class women. In order for upper-class wives to challenge their husbands' traditional economic role and its associated power in the family, they would have to ultimately challenge the men's economic role outside the family. These husbands are, after all, the men who manage the nation's business and financial affairs. It would mean a great deal, therefore, for wives to handle the family financial affairs. Mrs. Harper explained why she handed over her inheritance to her husband to manage, saying, "That is his field. He's in corporate finance." Mrs. Atherton said simply, "When it comes to investments, he's more qualified than I."

In other words, the women would ultimately have to challenge the men's class position in society in order to manage their own money. Upper-class men—as characterized in the introduction of this study—exercise the dominant economic and political power in the society. It is unlikely that they would relinquish such power in their own families or that their wives would be able to seriously challenge it. Sociologist Helen Hacker, as noted in chapter one, has claimed that since upper-class men have so much power in the wider society, they also have more power than other men at home in their marriages and families.[10] These points are considered further in the concluding chapter of this book.

There are other, less monumental, reasons why upper-class women do not significantly alter their position relative to their husbands. Ceretainly one factor is the presence of household help. Recall the comment of Mrs. Holt. When I asked how she and her husband divide household responsibilities, she said, "When you have someone else to do the work, there's not much dividing up to do." In the same vein, Mrs. Carnes (the young mother who had begun temporary part-time paid work) said that, although her husband is more involved in house and children than most, her full-time, live-in "girl" makes all the difference: "I couldn't have done this job without her. My husband hasn't noticed much change around the house [since I've been working] because of her." Unlike women of other classes, upper-class women can ease their household responsibilities with paid help. The impetus to alter their role at home is therefore less urgent.

Another factor is that women of the upper class, unlike their counterparts in other socioeconomic classes, are exempt from the economic necessity of working. This exemption is both an advantage and a disadvantage. Upper-class women need not take just any job to support themselves, and their children are not threatened by the feminization of poverty that is increasingly plaguing women and children today. But since they do not have to work, they lack that impetus to change their subordinate position at home. (Ironically, the upper-class husband may not have to work, for economic reasons, either; but he inevitably maintains an office outside the home and engages in some sort of work activity. And, according to the women I spoke with, he generally expects his wife to plan her time so his activities are not interfered with.)

Summary and Conclusions

The upper-class wife bears many similarities to traditional wives in other social classes. These similarities powerfully illustrate the subordinate position of women in society and the importance of gender frameworks as explanations for women's position in society. Even in the most priviledged class, women lack freedom, independence, and influence over family decisions relative to men.

Upper-class women, like other women, experience dissatisfaction with their role as wives—with its expected mode of accomodation, unequal voice in family decisions, and sole responsibility for home and family. But the obstacles they confront to changing their role are class-based and very different from the obstacles experienced by women in other classes.

Although the personal descriptions and expressions of the

role of the upper-class wife do not differ greatly from those of wives in other classes, the societal consequences are very different. A major consequence of upper-class wives' activities is to support the economic position of their husbands at the very top of society's hierarchy. As long as upper-class wives assume an accommodative and supportive function at home and in the community, their upper-class husbands are free to devote their full energies to managing the economic and political affairs of the society and to perpetuating the dominance of the upper class. As Dorothy Smith suggests, by supporting their husbands as individuals, upper-class women indirectly support and uphold the class structure.[11]

This view of the upper-class family as a central perpetuator of its own privilege is, of course, not a new one. In a study done over forty years ago, Warner and Lunt said that ". . . the upper class family . . . is a potent mechanism for maintaining the class system. . . . [It] maintains the values [of the class] and organizes the relations of its members."[12] Twenty-five years ago, Baltzell called attention to the importance of the traditional role of women in enhancing the continuity of the upper-class family—approving the fact that upper-class women are less likely than other women to have paid jobs. He asserts that this traditional position of women is an index of family stability," and he adds that, "On the whole, career women do not add to the stability of the home."[13] In contrast to the changes occurring in families of other classes, there has been little apparent change in the upper-class family. The great stability of the upper-class family was evidenced in a study of continuities and discontinuities in upper-class marriages by Paul Blumberg in 1975. Replicating a 1947 study by Hatch and Hatch, Blumberg found that "although tremendous forces have shaken American society in past generations, the upper class has retained itself remarkably intact, and, having done so, is perhaps the most untouched group in American life."[14]

To the extent that upper-class women are supportive of and

subjugated by this traditional family structure—with its rigid division of labor between the sexes and its traditional subordination of women—the function of the upper-class family is reinforced. As the primary social form for the orderly transmission of power and privilege from generation to generation, the family confines the women who preserve it.

Mother

4

"[My husband and I] followed the course that we grew up in. Our children were exposed to sports, music and the arts. They went to dancing school and learned the social graces and how to get along with the opposite sex. We sent them to camp, and the two who needed it, to boarding school."
(Mrs. Hammond)

Upper-class children are taught early that they are different from children of other socioeconomic classes. They learn that they have special talents and special responsibilities. Their association with children from other classes is limited, their individual abilities are nurtured, and their social responsibilities are disciplined. They are both protected and prodded so they can become the very best of what they can be, within the acceptable boundaries of class expectations. It is the task of their mothers, as the women themselves see it, to enforce these high standards of behavior and to structure children's participation in appropriate class activities and social organizations. Upper-class mothers take those responsibilities seriously, and they describe the expectations of motherhood with a strong awareness of what is required of them.

Expectations of Mothers

The importance of children to the upper class is first demonstrated by the number of children the women I spoke with had. Nearly eighty percent (28) of the women had three or more children; and one third (12) of the women had four or five children. The age of the women did not seem to make a difference. Other research has also shown that upper-class families tend to be larger than average. A recent text on social stratification based on a review of existing studies of the upper class reports that: "Children are valued as carriers of the family's elite status, and, accordingly, the number of children per family is considerably higher than in the middle class."[1]

In addition to sheer numbers, there is other evidence of the importance of children in the lives of these women. There are numerous descriptions of how they organize their lives to be at home when their children are. From these descriptions, it appears to be a myth that upper-class women leave the raising of children to hired caretakers. The proper development of the next generation of privilege is far too important to be left to hired hands. This is confirmed by Mrs. Wainwright, who said: "We don't have someone else taking care of our children. You've got to raise your own children if they're going to succeed."

In response to an open question about how they see their responsibilities as mothers, the women spoke most often of the importance of simply being there. Mrs. Eton, the mother of two grown boys, said, "I was always home when they got home." Mrs. Harper, a mother of five, qualified "being there" as most important when the children are small. She believes that mothers should be at home most of the time when children are little. During our interview, Mrs. Harper's youngest daughter arrived home for lunch from her nearby private day school. She went cheerfully to the kitchen to make her own peanut butter and jelly sandwich—apparently the universal food of American children, regardless of social class.

The women talked about how they arrange their own activities, particularly volunteer work, so that they can be home for their children. Mrs. Smythe (a mother of two school-age girls, and a woman particularly active in the community), said: "[A mother's] most important responsibility is to be on the scene until your child is six years old. There were things that I would have liked to be involved in before the girls were six, but I wouldn't do them."

Mrs. Holt (a mother of two grown children, and another particularly active community worker), reported: "I thought it was important that I be here when the children get home from school; I tried to arrange my volunteer work to be home in the afternoon." She was serious enough about her task as a mother to have taken several courses in child development when her children were small.

Mrs. Langdon, a mother of three related: "You have to arrange your time. I will not go to a meeting after my children are home. I know too many children who have gotten into trouble because they were left alone. I need to be here when the children get home. They need to talk. It's my most important role."

Mrs. Garson (an elderly woman who had raised two adopted children after the death of a birthchild) noted: "I didn't do any work that involved being away when the children were home for lunch. The children were the greatest thing in my life."

Mrs. Crowell (a young mother of three who is seriously contemplating a return to school for professional training and the eventual assumption of full-time work in her field) spoke of how she arranged her life to be at home for her three children:"I would not want to work full-time until my children were in high school. I turned down the presidency of [a women's political group] because I wanted to stay home with my last child. I found I had to do things nearby because I wanted to be home when my daughter was home. My priorities are with my family. I enjoy things outside, but not if they interfere with my family."

Mrs. Wilson spoke of what a job it had been to raise her four children. She thought that some women were not as well suited as she to motherhood: "Once you get past two children, it's a full-time job for a woman. I don't think too many people are going to have four kids. It's really more than anyone can do. It's hard work, and I think you should work hard at it. I try to be here when they get home from school. I feel women who don't do that are shirking their job. I have always arranged by activities so I'll be home."

Mrs. Wilson's comments are particularly interesting since she serves on the board of one of the city's oldest day care centers. When I asked her how she would feel about having her own children in such a center, she said she would have no trepidations about it. Given the statement she had made about mothers who are not at home with their children, this response did not seem entirely candid. I asked her, "You don't have any sense that they're really better off at home with their mothers?" She answered, "It depends on the kind of mothers they have." "Let's take you as a mother," I suggested. "Well," she replied, "I'm literate at least." This comment suggests that, like limitations on family size, centers for child care outside the home are viewed as being for children of other social classes—children whose mothers are seen to be less capable of properly caring for children than are upper-class mothers. This point of view is consistent with the many comments made in Chapter 2 on the meaning of class: there the women spoke of themselves as being "nicer people" and more responsible than others.

Some women appeared to genuinely enjoy the mother role

and to have made adjustments and accommodations that suited them, while not violating class norms for behavior. They had maximized the flexibility in the role-expectations of upper-class mother but had not seriously challenged them. Mrs. Hughes, for example, spoke of how her community work enhanced rather than detracted from her role as a mother: "I did volunteer work as much to be a better mother as anything else. I needed the stimulation outside the home when the children were small." Mrs. Howe agreed with Mrs. Hughes, saying, "I do a better job as a mother if I'm not here twenty-four hours a day."

Mrs. Carnes (the young mother who had just started a part-time paid job) had prioritized her work outside and inside the home. She said: "Working is okay as long as I put home and family first. I think I can do both." Mrs. Holt called attention to how it is possible for upper-class mothers, unlike their less affluent counterparts, *not* to be there twenty-four hours a day. Although Mrs. Holt, herself, was generally there by the time her children arrived home from school in the afternoons. She also said, "I was fortunate to have good help when my children were small, so that freed me to work in the community." Mrs. Cooper brings us back, however, to the norm for upper-class mothers—the norm that introduced this chapter: "If I have a child, it's my obligation to take care of it."

Some of the women found the demands of child-rearing especially heavy, and they expressed the conflicts they felt between their role as mothers and their work in the community. They were resigned to what they saw as a primary responsibility to children, yet some seemed to be counting the years until they would have more freedom. Mrs. Harper, for example, said: "I keep thinking in two more years the hours from eight-thirty to three-thirty will be my own. The [Junior] League expects women to be heavily involved between the ages of twenty-five and thirty-eight. Those are the years you should be home with your kids. It's a pretty full-time job, being there when they need you."

Mrs. Clarke said: "I'm home-centered now with this two-year-old. I miss seeing people, but it's what I wanted, to be there, to handle the problems day in and day out." Mrs. Lane is the extremely protective and cowed executive wife described in the last chapter, dependent on her husband's wealth since her own family had "lost everything in the crash of '29." She spoke poignantly, yet with a sense of ultimate submission, of her years as a young mother: "I was so unhappy in those first years with the children in diapers. I felt I was wasting my potential, but I adjusted to understanding that my family came first."

Mrs. Vincent was tempted by the possibly greater rewards of paid professional work over full-time motherhood. She said, nonetheless: "I am not willing to pursue what personally might be more satisfying to me, because my commitment to my family is greater than that to the community. It's equally rewarding to me to have people commend me on one of the children. I can't help but feel this reflects my contribution to the family." She, like the others, arranged her time around her children's school hours: "My hours [at home] are pretty much predestined. I have a child who comes home for lunch, so I've deferred making on-going commitments outside the home."

In sum, the statements of upper-class mothers place the highest priority on arranging time to spend with their children; they call attention to the fact that the upper-class mother is personally and intensively involved in the rearing of her own children, training them to meet class standards. In an effort to understand these standards, I asked the women what they want most for their children. What do they mean by "success" for their children?

Expectations of Children
Most of the women (over half) wanted their children to develop to their fullest potential. They want their children to be "the best," but claimed that they did not have any particular notions about

what the children had to be "the best" at. It is important, they said, that their children have a sense of accomplishment, self-satisfaction, and self-confidence. Mrs. Spears, mother of two sons, expressed this typical response articulately: "I want them to take something that's of interest to them and excel at it to the point of their potential. I don't want them to set levels so high that they feel as if they've failed if they don't reach them, but I do want them to make a positive contribution to society."

Mrs. Miles, a mother of four, now in her sixties, agreed with Mrs. Spears: "I want them to do their best. Success is doing something that needs doing, and doing it to your own satisfaction." Mrs. Nesbitt, also a mother of four and in her sixties, said, "I want my sons to realize their own ambitions, whatever they are." Mrs. Smythe, mother of two girls, spoke of the importance of how the children viewed themselves and what they did with their abilities: "I want them to have a sense of self-respect, to have a high value of themselves, and not to waste their talents."

However much the women themselves believed that they wanted only for their children to maximize their own potential— whatever that might be—they had some clearly class-defined notions of "success." Mrs. Ames, for example, said that as far as her children were concerned: "If you feel okay in yourself, that's all that really matters. Success would be if they're happy in what they're doing." Yet she spoke disapprovingly later in the interview of a son who is currently working in a rock band, saying: "I know he's capable of more. I wouldn't settle for that for him." Even more telling was her comment about another son: "My oldest son is there . . . he's successful. He's recognized as an up-and-coming young businessman, one of the fine young financial men in [the city]."

Mrs. Clarke reflected similar contradictions in a single statement of her view of success for her children: "To be stable and productive and accomplish what they want, a level of scholastic achievement, a liberal arts education, and then specialization in either business or medicine or law. Those are the traditional things."

She apparently saw no inconsistency in her wish that her children "accomplish what they want"—as long as it's "business or medicine or law." Most of the women, then, initially expressed the desire for their children to maximize their potential, to be the best of whatever it was they wanted to be. When pressed further, however, they often acknowledged, sometimes without realizing it themselves, their more specific and more limiting expectations. These expectations are consistent with the position of their class. They are of an assumed or "of course" nature, and the women did not seem to see any contradiction between their expectations and their initial statements. Illustrative of the taken-for-granted nature of their expectations was a comment by Mrs. Brownley, who said: "I suppose there is in each of us that desire to rise to the top. Of course [my children] will contribute to the community because they're responsible people. It's inevitable that they'll do that."

Like Mrs. Brownley, the women want their children to be seen as people who "contribute to the community." Mrs. Sharpe, whose family name was well known in the city, said: "I've tried so hard to tell them that I expect they will contribute to the organizations my family has been involved in for three generations. It's very important to me that they have a sense of responsibility to the community." Mrs. Haines made another typical comment: "I really believe in noblesse oblige. I think my girls are being brought up in as fortunate a position as I was. When I was eighteen, I was told I had to spend afternoons at the hospital. I hope to bring my girls up so they want to do the same."

A major component of their expectations for their children is the women's own experience of growing up. Recall, in Chapter 1, what they said about the pressures of living up to a family name, of the burdensome obligations of being expected to contribute to the community. Despite their reservations, however, it is this sense of obligation, of "social responsibility," that they want their children to carry on as they have.

When I asked the women what specific activities they encouraged for their children, they frequently mentioned athletics. Mrs. Spears (who had said she wanted her children to "excel to the extent of their potential") talked about the importance of sports in learning to deal with challenge. She said: "They all participated in athletics with vigor. I felt it was a challenge to them. The boys still can't beat me in tennis. They have so much drive and energy that they need an outlet." Mrs. Martin, mother of five, spoke of how sports enhance ones sense of self and keep one active: "Athletics [are] important. I think they build confidence and it's a commitment to lifetime activity."

Mrs. Atherton, mother of four, spoke of the importance of learning to compete through athletics, and of how one son had run counter to his father's views of what sports were appropriate for him: "My husband felt that sports were a great character builder, and he is a hell of a competitor so he was anxious for his son to do the same. Our son is taking modern dance now, and it's taken my husband a long time to accept that."

Several of the women voluntarily denied the importance of the competitive aspect of sports and highlighted other reasons they thought sports were important for their children. Mrs. Langdon, a mother of three, said: "Athletics are important. It teaches them how to control their bodies. I don't believe in competition though. I want them to learn sportsmanship instead of how to compete." Mrs. Vincent (the mother of four who had said that she wanted her children to be able to stand on their own two feet and to be content with what they were doing) said, "I've encouraged them to be in sports, but we're not competitive."

Closely related to the importance of athletics is the seriousness with which some of the women take their children's play activities. Mrs. Howe, for example described her approach: "We expose the boys to as broad a range of activities as possible, and from that they choose what they're interested in individually. They really have to be very interested in something before we'll support it, but then we'll go all the way with them. For example, our youngest is interested in magic, so we've given him all the books and materials he needs to become a crackerjack magician." A comparable theme was expressed by Mrs. Farley, who wants her children to dedicate themselves to specific projects: "I did encourage each one of them to have some kind of project, and I've encouraged each to have some outdoor sport."

Sports and the arts—even the phase of being interested in magic, which many children seem to pass through—are taken very seriously by upper-class mothers. They are not simply opportunities for recreation and enjoyment; they are also opportunities for training and learning to do one's best. They develop the characteristics considered important for upper-class children's success—characteristics such as the willingness to meet a challenge, self-confidence, control, competitiveness, performing at one's peak level, discipline and the ability to see a project through to the end.

Upper-class mothers, like all mothers, worry about their children abusing drugs and sex. When I asked the women what they saw to be the worst problem with their children, they replied that the hardest thing for them to accept or to deal with—in actuality or hypothetically—would be the use of drugs. This was mentioned by one fourth of the women. The concern about drug involvement reflected a general fear of their children becoming involved in what the women saw as the highly undesirable values and behavior of the counterculture of the late sixties and early seventies. They spoke in hushed tones of these times; and the mothers whose children had escaped those frightening years unharmed were most grateful.

Mrs. Hoight spoke of her fears for her three children: "It would really shake me up if they became totally involved in the drug culture and the hippie culture, if they vanished into the darkness of a commune. I know people that that's happened to and I think they're wrecking their lives. I know my boys have smoked marijuana and there's nothing I can do about it. I suggest to them that I think it's a rotten habit and I have made a big issue of it, but there's not really much you can do with a twenty year old boy. I don't want a bunch of illegitimate children around either, and there's also not much I can do about that."

Mrs. Wilson expressed her greatest worry for her four children: "We worry about the drug thing a good deal. I think that's the worst. It scares me more than anything. As far as sex is concerned, you've just go to roll with the punches, but dope . . . that's the most frightening. I know our two older girls have tried marijuana. We know families where their children's lives have been literally ruined by drugs, people who used LSD, who have been in mental institutions for months. I don't think it's really much of a possibility with our kids. If their money started going for that, we'd know it immediately. We've argued it all out, whether it's harmful or not. I'm one hundred percent against it. My husband is more broadminded. He says let them try it. We let them have alcohol at home. I'd rather have them drink than use marijuana. It's a known quantity, and it's temporary."

Mrs. Smythe, whose teenage daughter had actually been involved in a recent episode with marijuana, described how it affected her and the family: "She was expelled from [a private day school in the city] for having marijuana at school. That was a bitter blow, as hard a thing that ever happened to us. It's the sort of thing that happens to someone else. We tried to make it clear that although we were very opposed to what she did we still loved her. She lost all her friends. Fortunately, they were willing to take her at [the other private day school in the city]. The reason we didn't send her to public school was because there's a lot of marijuana use there, and that was the last thing she needed then." The Smythe girl apparently had the support and love of her family, if not her peers. No punitive family measures were mentioned.

In contrast, Mrs. Wainwright described her son's experience

and the reaction of his grandfather, the family patriarch: "I don't think the family has been very tolerant. There was a time when [my father-in-law] was so displeased with my oldest boy. . . . His first fault was that he didn't make good marks. He has long hair, and he did get involved with drugs, and he doesn't have a job. These things are just anathema [to my husband's family]. He was the first grandchild and his grandfather tried to raise him. He's stopped giving the annual gift to my son, primarily because of the long hair and the beard."

Mrs. Wainwright's father-in-law was not alone in his use of the family money to keep the children in line. When I asked Mrs. Appleton what the worst problem would be for her in regard to her children, she said, "Oh, I guess if they shot somebody, got in trouble with the law." Her son was munching on a sandwich at the other side of the large family kitchen in which we were sitting. Though his head was ostensibly buried in a book, he looked up quickly and snapped at his mother: "Ha! How about if we dropped out of school?" She shot him a warning glance, and I pressed on. I asked what she would do if the children engaged in "unacceptable" behavior. Her son, apparently not cowed by her warning, retorted before she could answer: "You'd cut off the money, wouldn't you, Mom?" His mother blushed noticeably, and then went on as if he had not spoken.

Mrs. Wilson, in another instance of using money to control the children, was about to travel across the country to visit her daughter who was threatening to drop out of college. She said the intention of her maternal visit was to "pull on the purse strings a little." Though many parents use money to exert a certain amount of control over children, this type of discipline seems especially well-suited to an affluent class.

Besides being concerned that their children avoid negative behaviors, upper-class mothers also want to ensure that their children have positive opportunities and experiences. One of the most important of these is a good education. Most upper-class mothers I spoke with agreed with Mrs. Hammond, who said that: "A good education is most basic. You should give your children the best education you can." Mrs. Wainwright agreed and saw this as related to social responsibility: "We wanted education for our children most of all. We wanted them to have trained minds and make a contribution."

The importance of a good education was expressed by the number of women who mentioned children's problems in school as the most difficult issue they had to deal with. Mrs. Clarke (the young mother who said that what she wanted most for her children was "a level of scholastic achievement") described the worst problem she could have: "We've tackled them, the scholastic problems. My son was at the bottom of the barrel in second grade. Now he's in special schools, and doing well."

Mrs. Lane, a mother with three grown children, also answered this question in terms of her son's doing poorly in school: "My son had problems in school because his father was on the board. He had no self-confidence and blamed his father's position for everything. I think I was too understanding. I think I should have pushed him more to accomplish something. I should have been stricter, tougher."

Mrs. Carpenter, who has no children, blamed the schools for a wide range of perceived problems with children during the decade of the seventies. "Children of friends of mine who were in college at the time of [the] Kent State [killings] are not normal even now. It was a hard time and I blame it on the education system. I know some of the teachers were communist, and I think the parents were too permissive too. I know several teachers like that at [the local private day school] and I recommended that they be fired."

It is hardly surprising that upper-class mothers want quality education for their children; but this, like the matter of maximizing potential, has a special twist for their children. A quality education, by definition, means private, upper-class schools. The women described these schools as "independent" schools. This category includes the exclusive, costly day schools located in the city in which this study was conducted, as well as the eastern boarding schools known for their upper-class clientele, such as: Exeter, Hotchkiss, Milton, and Choate, for the boys; Madiera, Dobbs Ferry, Miss Porter's and Miss Hall's, for the girls.

As with other things these women wanted for their children, attending private school was a repetition of their own pattern. Mrs. Wilson said: "I went to private school, and I think you get a better education there. We can afford it." The other women were also convinced that their children received a better education in private schools. Mrs. Howe, for example, said: "Since we can afford it, we want them to have the best education possible." Mrs. Carnes concurred, saying, "They get the best education there." Mrs. Langdon specified small classes and the quantity of homework as the reasons why she believed her children got a better education in private school, noting, "There are smaller classes, more outside work."

Most of the women I spoke with had sent their children to one of three private upper-class day schools in the city. Boarding schools, as opposed to private day schools, are not as typical of the class as they once were.[2] Ten of the women, however, followed the older pattern: they had sent their children to boarding schools that, without exception, were listed by earlier studies as upper-class schools.[3] Five of these women are now in their fifties or older and their children are grown; the other five are younger women with children currently in school.

There appear to be two reasons for sending children to boarding schools rather than to private day schools: first, if a child has what their family considers to be a problem, either academic or personal/social, and is in need of special attention; second, if attendance at a particular boarding school is a family tradition. Mrs.

Hammond, a mother of five children, two of whom had gone to boarding school, illustrates the first of these reasons. She said: "One of them went because he liked the ladies more than he liked school. The other went because he was smaller than the other boys his age and he needed a year to catch up."

Similarly, Mrs. Miles explained why she sent one of her daughters to the same eastern boarding school that she had attended: "She was a very shy child. She'd prefer to stay at home than to see her contemporaries in town. She didn't date and do things the other girls did, so I thought that from the age of fifteen to eighteen going away to school would be good for her, would give her some confidence and put her on her feet."

While Mrs. Hammond and Mrs. Miles described reasons of personal adjustment for sending their children to boarding school, Mrs. Wilson and Mrs. Brownley called attention to academic reasons. Mrs. Wilson said: "We sent one of our girls away to boarding school because she wasn't doing well here." Mrs. Brownley made a similar comment: "[Boarding school] was especially important for our son since he was not a very good student." Upper-class children, including those who are admittedly poor students, are simply not allowed to fail academically or personally. This gives them striking advantages over children of other classes.

Mrs. Wainwright emphasized a family tradition of three generations as the main reason that her sons went to boarding school: "My husband wanted to repeat his educational history. He went to junior high in the public system and then on to ———. His father [my son's grandfather] had gone to ——— too, and [the grandfather] had the expectation that all of his grandchildren would go there." Family tradition was also the main reason that Mrs. Appleton sent her children to boarding school. She also noted the advantage of expanding their social network beyond the city where they lived: "They went to boarding school because my husband and I went, and because you meet people there from all over."

Particular boarding schools are, thus, one of the traditions that upper-class families maintain—a tradition often passed along with wealth, from generation to generation, enhancing the stability of the class.

Women spoke of the social as well as the educational advantages of private schools. Private schools serve to build the social networks among the upper class; and they set upper-class children off from children of other social classes. Mrs. Wainwright said frankly and succinctly: "You don't go to private school just for your education. You go there to be separated from ordinary people." Mrs. Langdon described what she thought her children might have to put up with if they went to school with "ordinary people": "I don't want my children to be exposed to the things that go on in public schools, drugs and vandalism."

Mrs. Appleton had built social networks in school that were useful to her in later life in gaining access to upper-class organizations. She wanted this advantage for her children: "Where I went to boarding school, there were girls from all over the country, so I know people from all over. It's helpful when you move to a new city and want to get invited into the local social club." Attendance at upper-class schools is, thus, one way that members of the upper-class create and maintain the exclusivity of their way of life and their social interactions. The women I interviewed were cognizant of these class functions of private schools and fully supported them as necessary for their children's well-being.

In addition to maximizing potential within acceptable class boundaries, contributing to the community and getting a good education at an upper class private school, what the women I talked with wanted most for their children was a "compatible" marriage. A typical response reflecting concern for the future family life of her children was made by Mrs. Wilson, who said: "I hope my children will marry someone they have interests in common with. It makes life a lot easier."

Most parents have this same hope for their children. But the upper-class version, again, has a particular twist. For the women I spoke with, a "compatible marriage" is, first and foremost, a marriage within their own class. I discovered this class-bound meaning of compatible marriage most conclusively when I asked the women about the particular activities they encourage for their children. Schooling and the building of same-sex networks are complemented by activities that build the appropriate other-sex networks. For the youngest children, this means attending the right dancing schools. For the older children, it means participating in recreational activities and organizations whose membership is by invitation only. These activities eventually lead to the society debut for upper-class girls and their escorts.

The most frequently mentioned reason for wanting children to participate in society debuts—and the activities and organizations leading to them—is the opportunity to meet, and eventually marry, acceptable members of the other sex. Mrs. Harper said: "It started as a way of putting the boys and girls together. I think the only reason it's lasted is because the private schools separate boys and girls so they don't have the opportunity to meet each other."

Mrs. Hammond felt that the debut was most important to announce her daughter's availability for marriage: "The [debutante ball] is more important for girls. You don't introduce a boy to society the way you do a girl. It goes back to saying 'Here is my daughter. She is now eighteen and ready for marriage.' "

Mrs. Hoight found the dancing school/debut track to be the place where "the boys might meet girls," a place to meet acceptable partners for an eventual acceptable marriage. Mrs. Holt, a mother of two, added: "It's a way to meet people. If my children hadn't gone to [sex-segregated] independent schools, if they'd had other chances to meet members of the opposite sex, maybe it wouldn't have been so important."

Mrs. Martin (who expressed the desire for "a good marriage

that will last" as her major hope for her children) said of the debut activities her sons had recently taken part in: "I thought they needed to do it because they didn't meet any girls at school." When asked about the function of dancing classes for her young sons, Mrs. Howe said typically, "Well, they don't have many other opportunities to meet girls."

The women were explicit about the exclusive nature of these activities. Mrs. Cooper, mother of four, said, "They meet some nice people, the same kind of kids getting together." Mrs. Harper, who had recently taken her turn chairing the committee that runs the annual debut, described how class exclusivity is maintained: "It's a lot of busy work for one evening's fun. It has absolutely no value at all and does nothing for the city. It's a strictly social function, a very select, invitational group. The parties are safe. People you don't know can't crash. It's a carefully checked list. You try to match names so you don't get people just off the streets."

These comments imply what upper-class mothers hope for the marriages of their children. When I asked Mrs. Smythe what kind of marriage she would want for her two young daughters, she said, "I'm stuffy enough to dislike people who don't have manners, people who aren't interested in the arts and in their community."

The importance of a class-compatible marriage also came up in response to the question, later in the interview, of what the hardest problem would be in relation to children. Mrs. Hall (the mother of four who had claimed earlier that what she wanted most for her children was a happy family life) said that the greatest problem for her would be ". . . if the children married someone I didn't like." Several women were particularly concerned about the possibility of their children entering an interracial marriage. In response to this same question, Mrs. Holt said: "I certainly wouldn't abandon them if they married someone I didn't approve of, a Black person or whatever, but it would be difficult. It's easier to marry somebody near your own interests and background. It makes for compatibility." Mrs. Miles, whose daughter had in fact been romantically involved with a man not of her race, said: "This involvement of my daughter's was the worst for me. I told her I would hope you would decide not to marry this man, that marriage is problematic enough without a difference in race, religion and background."

Mrs. Cooper expressed concern about interracial marriage, but claimed to be more accepting of a religious difference: "I think it would be very hard for me if one of them married a Black. Two of my sons dated very nice Jewish girls, and I think that would be something I could live with."

Mrs. Nesbitt's son had married outside his class. She told of the sad ending of this marriage, which, she claimed, she had not initially opposed: "[My daughter-in-law's family] hadn't had anything, but we judged her on her own merits. I thought she could bridge anything, but I was wrong. I think she felt we didn't understand her, which was not true. She used to say we couldn't imagine what it was to have nothing. She had a terrible inferiority complex. It's difficult to overcome that difference in background." Note the *class* explanation that Mrs. Nesbitt gives for the failure of her son's marriage—a sort of explanation that provides evidence for the importance of the class frame that those upper-class women so often use to make sense of their own lives.

Thus, upper-class women consider a vital part of their role as mothers to be the need to maximize opportunities for class marriages. They do this by constructing class-exclusive social organizations and activities, where upper-class boys and girls can meet one another. These organizations, as Mrs. Hughes said, are "run by women, mothers." They are important for their children's personal happiness; and the social consequences—in terms of maintaining the integrity and coherence of the upper class—are direct and essential to perpetuating the class.

Debut activities are also important in other ways. When I

asked the women why they encouraged their children to take part in such activities, they mentioned family tradition almost as frequently as class marriage. Mrs. Hughes, a woman from one of the city's oldest families, said, for example: "My mother was one of the women who started [the debutante ball] so I felt the children should do it whether they wanted to or not." Mrs. Wilson, also from an old family, spoke similarly: "We only did it for [the children's] grandmother. I think it's passé, and I don't care about it, but it's just something that's done. I'm a product of my family background.

Mrs. Farley's daughter had made her debut for family reasons as well. Mrs. Farley also recognized that a function of the debut was to "maintain the family's image"—society's view of the family's social and class standing. She said: "[My daughter's] dad wanted her to do it. We do have a family image to maintain. It was important to the grandparents, and I felt it was an obligation to her family to do it."

Mrs. Brownley, who also emphasized the role of family tradition, seemed somewhat defensive about her daughter's participation. She tried to downplay its significance: "It was a heritage thing. My husband's mother and sisters had done it. It's an occasion to introduce your daughter to your mature friends. I know this sort of thing is somewhat outmoded. It's really pure snobbery. It's not going to improve their position any or change or improve them as people. It's not a necessity just a social form I subscribe to."

The debut and the organizational activities leading to it also provide opportunities for upper-class children to learn the manners and social graces that set them off from children of other social classes. These social graces are not just optional amenities of upper-class life; they are essential to the ways in which the upper-class persons are able to control—with great civility and charm—virtually any social situation in which they find themselves. The upper class does not, of course, have a monopoly on pleasantries conducive to social intercourse; but they do seem to be better trained in social intricacies and, thus, have clear social advantages. Speaking of the importance of the dancing classes and invitational youth groups, Mrs. Howe said: "It's just good old-fashioned manners, how to put people at ease. We hope the boys will be comfortable in any social setting. They may find themselves in situations where a certain touch of class is called for, and we don't want them to be uncomfortable." Mrs. Harper, who had recently chaired the major debutante event, said, "It's a way to put in a little gentleness, and a little manners." And Mrs. Clarke's young children were now attending the dancing classes that would lead eventually to the debut "so they would know how to act at formal occasions, how to dance."

The invitational nature of these activities is central to their social meaning. The importance of debut activities is fundamentally rooted in the quality of exclusiveness. Mrs. Smythe offered, frankly, that participation in debutante activities was important for women of this class to succeed in their roles as community volunteers. When I asked her how her two daughters might benefit from making their debut, she said: "Well, it's very helpful when you're raising money in the community to be socially accepted, to have the stamp of approval." Mrs. Harper also described the debut as a mark of acceptance: "It's strictly a social function. For many families, it's a great social step to be accepted."

Exclusivity inevitably means that there are some who are left out. Mrs. Spears described her feelings about this: "It's impossible to include everybody in the world in your social life. I have tried to not in any way discriminate against anybody, but on the other hand there is something such as congeniality."

Mrs. Harper had not been able to justify this kind of exclusion as well as Mrs. Spears. She did not deny its necessity, but did not want to be personally involved, saying: "I hate to think about who gets in and who stays out. I don't want any part of deciding that." Mrs. Smythe, whose two young girls will make their debuts when the time comes, recognizes the pain that those left out must feel: "Once you belong, it doesn't mean very much. It's only when you can't that it hurts."

Mrs. Carnes, who had been the first in her family to be invited to a debut, also notes the price of exclusiveness to those on the outside looking in: "I enjoyed the ball. I think I did it for my parents. If they still have it when my girls are in college, I expect we'll do it. When I did it, a lot of my friends didn't, and I know they felt shut out. My mother said I could poo-poo it all I wanted because I was in and it was easy to criticize when I had it."

One way of dealing with exclusion from an event is to stage an event of one's own. Mrs. Atherton described how she and other "newcomers" had established their own debutante ball called the Cotillion as an alternative to the established assembly—and how she learned that letting people in also meant closing others out: "When the Cotillion society was formed, I was asked to chair the first ball. It's a group comparable to [the assembly] except it's not the first families of the city. I think at the time I thought my chairing the ball would enhance our position in the community, and I was delighted to be asked. I became terribly turned off by how new members were chosen. There was a membership committee who could black-ball anybody. I suffered a lot of guilt about that, but we're still members because the group does raise money for scholarships."

Exclusivity as a way of life means that some people are "in" and others are "out." Upper-class women are often aware of the painful nature of being "left out"; but they do not generally question class exclusiveness, which for them, is a "natural" style of living. This topic is discussed further in the next chapter in relation to upper-class clubs.

Several women denied the importance of the debutante ball and the organizational activities leading to it, though they and their children had participated. Mrs. Hughes said: "It was of no importance whatsoever. It was just something we had to do." Mrs. Garson agreed: "It wasn't terribly important, but it was an expected part of growing up. It's a social value."

Countering these verbal protests, a number of mothers (seven of the women I interviewed) claimed that they had insisted their children participate in debut activities even though the children objected. Mrs. Martin, a mother of five, realized that her children "hated it, but it was just part of my background. They did what was right." Mrs. Hoight, who thought her sons might meet suitable future wives in the social activities leading to the debut, acknowledged that she "made the kids go. I told them they had to do it."

Mrs. Cooper (who had described the importance of these activities as "the same kind of kids getting together") also notes that her children "hated every minute of it, but they met some nice people." Mrs. Chambers, mother of a thirteen-year-old girl currently in an exclusive dancing class, said: "She says she doesn't like it, but I know she does. It's a negative form of rebellion not to participate. To refuse to participate is just dumb. She'd miss a lot of fun. It's a tradition, something you do. Nobody in my generation ever questioned it."

Why would these women deny the importance of something of such consequence to them that they insist their children do it even over the children's objections? A clue is found in the somewhat defensive comment made by Mrs. Brownley earlier in this section: playing down the significance of the debut she called it class "snobbery." Mrs. Brownley, like many of the other women in this study seems to recognize that people of other classes are offended, sometimes angered, by the exclusivity of upper-class organizations and activities—indeed, perhaps, by the very existence of such a wealthy and powerful class in a democratic society. Comments reported in Chapter 2 indicate that some of the women are aware of the hostility of other classes.

Many activities of the upper-class—such as most activities of clubs and schools and those within the family—are relatively invisible to members of other classes. Other activities, like community volunteerism, are intended to pay back the community and society for the privileges that the upper class knowingly possess. There is, obviously, no need to play down activities that are invisible to other classes or those that claim to contribute to the public good. Society debuts are somewhat different.

Debuts are more public than most upper-class activities. As annual events, they are much glamorized and romanticized in the media and in fictional accounts of upper-class life. In the city where this study was conducted, nearly an entire page of the major newspaper is devoted each year to the pictures and names of the young women who "come out." (It is one of the rare times that these old families seek out press coverage.) In the year of this study, an angry letter to the editor followed the publication of a special Sunday section of the newspaper covering the year's upper-class debutante ball. The writer objected to the coverage, saying: "I see nothing newsworthy about the annual Ball, held at that bastion of the privileged class, the————Club. Other than the participants and their relatives, who is the least interested in the doings of these so-called prominent families and their vapid debutante daughters?"

This comment shows considerable naiveté about the important social consequences of the debut and of other, apparently empty, social forms of upper-class life. It also clearly shows resentment of the class and its privileges. Members of the upper class are aware of such resentment, and they protect themselves against it when talking with outsiders by minimizing the importance of the more public upper-class rituals. The women I interviewed may have been doing just this when they spoke with me about the lack of importance of the social debut, a rite of passage for upper-class children into adulthood.

The debut is also an opportunity for public recognition and class acceptance of newcomers (such as the Hammond's daughter,

Mrs. Carnes) and for the exclusion of unacceptable persons. Though some of the mothers who run these functions want nothing to do with the "dirty work" of sorting out the "acceptables," from the "unacceptables," they all see this as an unavoidable fact of life.

Thus from early dancing classes to the once-in-a-lifetime debutante ball, upper-class children are expected to take part in the patterns of upper-class life. And, for the most part, they do so. As social scientists have long known, social forms, however empty they may appear in content, are essential to the patterning of social life and the maintenance of social groups. These forms are the expression of social structure in everyday life created and upheld by participants who describe it as "natural," "just something you do".

Summary and Conclusions

On the surface, upper-class mothers appear to want for their children what mothers of other social classes want for theirs—the chance to become the best they can be, to contribute to the community in some way, to develop life-long, enjoyable leisure pursuits, to stay out of trouble, to get a good education, and to have happy marriages. But each of these hopes and expectations has a meaning specific to the upper-class context.

Mothers in the upper class want their children to be the best of what they can be, but acceptable occupations fall within the confines of the major professions and top of the corporate world. They want their children to contribute to the community, as shown in Chapter 6, within the context of noblesse oblige—the responsibility to help the less fortunate and to return some of their own great wealth and privilege to those who lack it. The children's games and other activities are training grounds for discipline, competition, confidence and a sense of control. Staying out of trouble is contained, ultimately, by threats of losing the family inheritance. A good education means an education at a private, upper-class school, which implies not only the best possible academic training but also invaluable social networks. A happy marriage means a class-compatible marriage, which maintains the integrity and stability of the class and produces children who will begin the cycle all over again.

While some of these expectations might be shared by parents of other social classes, upper-class parents are able to provide the special advantages that maximize their children's chances of living up to these expectations. Wanting one's child to be a major figure in business or law is not unique to upper-class parents; nor is wanting one's child to use recreational pursuits to learn self-confidence; nor is wanting one's child to stay out of trouble. But when these expectations are placed in the context of real advantages—such as access to private schools, upper-class recreational groups, and exclusive networks—then the whole "package" becomes class-specific. And it is a package that children of other classes cannot hope to match.

Two other features stand out in an analysis of upper-class mother's: The first is that they want their children to have what they had themselves; to repeat their own experience. As Mrs. Hammond said: "You see it's really what you did yourself that you want your children to do."

This differs from the desire of parents of other social classes. Upward social mobility in America leads many parents to want their children to achieve and acquire what they themselves could not. Studies by sociologists Richard Sennett and Lillian Breslow Rubin suggest that this is particularly true of the working class.[4] The upper class is already at the top: the maintenance of their position, not upward-striving, is the issue for them. They want their children to carry on and to protect what they have already accomplished and acquired in past generations.

Second, for upper-class mothers, there is an obvious link between the personal and the social—what is necessary for their children's individual happiness and what is objectively necessary for the perpetuation of the class. As the children maximize their individual potential, they also fill the positions at the top of the economic hierarchy that perpetuates the wealth and power of their class. As the children contribute to the community, in the tradition of social responsibility, they also protect their privilege (as Chapter 6 will show) from serious challenges. As the children enjoy the opportunities of quality education, they also acquire academic and social advantages that are, for the most part, not available to other children—thereby enhancing their potential and exercising their influence in the community and in society. As the children enter class-compatible marriages, they also maintain the class as a distinct social and economic entity—and pass wealth, privilege, and a way of life on to the next generation. Thus, for upper-class children, doing what they want to do for personal happiness and doing what they should do to construct and maintain a social class are especially consonant with one another. And their mothers are primarily responsible for creating and upholding this consonance and the expectations and activities to which it leads and which it, in turn, creates.

Dissonance is not completely absent: mothers of the upper-class sometimes chafe under the demands of parenthood, and their children are not always willing to do what they're supposed to do. But, overall, the role of the upper class mother seems a very stable one. Like the role of wife, it has not been much affected by the changes that mothers in other social classes have undergone and, in some instances, sought. The stability of the role, like that of wife, is necessary to maintain the class in its current form—passing on to each generation of privilege a sense of entitlement, the cultural advantages necessary for success, and access to the exclusive social networks that support its influence in the larger society. An important aspect of the upper-class network—exclusive clubs—will be discussed in the next chapter.

Club
Member

5

"The club is a place to go where you can have lunch and discuss business without having to wade through the mass of people. You want to have people who are congenial, all the same social group." (Mrs. Harper)

"If I go out to the club to relax, I don't want people around I don't care about. Sameness, homogeneity—they're very pleasant." (Mrs. Lane)

The previous chapter examined the role of exclusive social organizations and activities for upper class children. This chapter concentrates on the major exclusive organization for the adults—the upper-class club. Virtually everyone who has studied the upper class has recognized the importance of the club in creating and maintaining upper class social networks. Membership in identifiably upper-class clubs has long been considered a valid indicator of upper-class membership.[1] But few have talked directly with upper class persons themselves about these clubs, even fewer with women in particular.

As the comments of Mrs. Harper and Mrs. Lane indicate, a central feature of upper-class clubs is their highly select membership. This feature screens out unacceptable people—people whom Mrs. Lane "didn't care about," people Mrs. Harper called "the mass." Acceptable people are those considered to be like themselves, people seen as "congenial" or "part of the same social group."

To some degree all of us prefer to associate with others like ourselves, people with similar interests and values. Early evidence of the homogeneity of association comes from community studies such as the Lynds' studies of Middletown, Warner and Lunt's study of Yankee City, and Hollingshead's study of Elmtown.[2] A review of these studies led Mayer and Buckley to conclude over ten years ago that, "in these various communities . . . , individuals and families confine their social relationships, particularly the more intimate ones, largely to others with similar cultural characteristics."[3] Exclusivity of association is, then, not unique to the upper class; but, as this chapter will show, the exclusivity of upper-class clubs has specific social consequences unlike those of social relations in other classes.

It was an unquestioned fact of life that membership in such clubs is by invitation only. Mrs. Lane preceded the statement quoted above by saying, "I'm glad [the club] is invitational." This aspect of upper-class life is so taken for granted that the women have difficulty imagining an alternative way of going about things— with the exception of the newcomers.

Mrs. Atherton and Mrs. Nesbitt, both newcomers, responded with objections to my question about the importance of invitational membership in these clubs. Mrs. Atherton said: "I don't think they should be invitational. I think an income level would be enough of a criterion." Note that she did not object to the exclusivity of the clubs, but to the method and criteria for selection. Mrs. Nesbitt also objected to membership by invitation only: "So many of the things [in this city] are invitational. That's not the way it was in [the city where we lived before]. I think it makes this city decadent. I've brought this up to my friends here many times, but they're blind to it. My husband and I joined because we needed some way to make friends."

Mrs. Atherton and Mrs. Nesbitt were exceptions to the rule. No doubt, they objected to the invitational selection not because of its exclusivity, per se, but because of the process that they had to go through to get accepted. By contrast, women from the old families were accepted much more automatically; and they were unanimous in their approval of membership by invitation. It is, they felt, the only way to keep upper-class clubs "compatible" or "congenial," terms used almost universally.

Mrs. Martin, for example, spoke about the importance of invitational membership: "People come together because of a community of interests and outlook. Because the city is large and the people who are active in the community come from a variety of backgrounds, there is pressure to enlarge the membership, but I believe in the right of association. What binds [the clubs] together and makes them pleasant is the common interests and outlook. I'm not sure how much sense it would make to bring in people who are not congenial."

Mrs. Wright agreed, even though her husband, who is a Jew, has for many years been excluded from membership in the clubs to which his wife and her family belong. She said in support of invitational membership: "I think your social life is with the people you choose, a certain group, those you would have to your home, people who are congenial."

Who, I wondered, had to be kept out of the clubs? Why was the invitational membership process so generally accepted among the upper class? And what, beyond congeniality, was the justification for such exclusion? The people the women screened out, people they considered to be unacceptable, were initially described in broad terms—"everybody" or "just anybody." Mrs. Smythe, for example, said: "It's the psychology of exclusiveness. People like to belong to things that everybody can't belong to."

Mrs. Farley and Mrs. Sharpe spoke in disparaging terms of the open membership of the local women's club. Mrs. Farley said: "Some people [like myself] think you should be able to choose whom you associate with. Otherwise you're going to be like [the women's city club] where everybody's a member." Mrs. Sharpe implied that if the upper-class women's club had a more open membership, their programs, such as lectures, would decline in quality: "If people just want to go to a lecture in a vague enough area to take care of practically anybody who comes, that club is there." Her comment provided the beginnings of a justification for keeping out the "anybodies." This justification had already been expressed in the interviews. It is the belief that upper-class women are somehow better than other people, and thus more deserving and better able to take advantage of their special privileges.

Mrs. Lane (who was quoted as saying that the invitational feature of upper-class clubs was important in keeping out the people she didn't "care about") specified some qualities of acceptable people, people whom she did "care about": "I like having people like myself around, quiet, conservative, nice to their children, who don't run around with others' wives, and are interested in the community."

Like Mrs. Lane, Mrs. Langdon defined her class equals as "nice people." She said: "If you're a nice person, compatible with the rest of the group, I think you can get into all of these clubs. I mean interested in your family or in their activities; not interested in showing off a certain standard of living, not competitive. We quit a club that was like that, where winning at tennis was the important thing."

Who were the people who weren't "compatible," who weren't "nice" enough? When I asked Mrs. Atherton about the criteria for getting into the upper-class clubs, she said first: "Well, of course there's racial discrimination. That's the biggest. Then there're religious differences." Most of the women I talked with referred in some way to racial and religious criteria for club membership, though few were as explicit as Mrs. Atherton.

Mrs. Brownley spoke in critical terms, for example, of the current admissions policy of the Junior League. The Junior League is a national service organization for women. It is invitational and has many of the qualities of an upper-class social club, as well as being a prototype of the serious volunteerism discussed in the next chapter. According to Mrs. Brownley, the new policy of the League was to take "just anybody." She spoke with nostalgia and some annoyance of the "good old days" of greater exclusiveness by race and religion. Using the apparent rationale of controlling the size of the organization, she said: "It was closed in the sense that we didn't invite colored people or Jewish people. I suppose with this new openness, they can grow until they can't find a place big enough to hold meetings. Their new policy is to take anybody that's presented, and that means Indians, Africans, Alaskans, anybody."

Mrs. Harper spoke in similar terms, though she specified the qualities of an acceptable Black: "[The League is] taking in Blacks, Jews, anybody now, whereas it used to be all white Protestant. I was in the League when we took in the first Black, and I don't think there was a big debate about it. She's an outstanding gal, and there [doesn't] seem to be any more who want to join. The Blacks I know wear their Black awareness proudly and I don't think they want to join. This woman we admitted is more interested in general welfare than she is about raising the cause of Blacks. There haven't been others applying. They have their own Black group."

For Blacks to be acceptable, then, they must put the "general" interest ahead of that of their own race. "Acceptable" Blacks are also defined as rather suspect in terms of loyalty to their own race. Their membership in predominantly white clubs is seen as calling their "racial pride" into question. And, while an occasional "outstanding" Black may be accepted into an upper-class club or organization, it is clear that significant numbers of them will not be allowed.

Racial and religious exclusion were described in the context of three commonly used rationalizations for prejudice and discrimination. Mrs. Martin exemplified the first form of rationalization, which is that it's all right to discriminate since Blacks and Jews discriminate too: "Differences can exist among Blacks and Jews as well. I understand that Jewish people are very strict about membership in their clubs. They have restrictions about membership in their clubs that we might not approve of at all."

Mrs. Carpenter illustrated another common rationalization, which is that, while she herself is not prejudiced, others in her group object to Blacks and Jews and need to have their opinions respected. She said: "I wouldn't oppose the admission of Blacks or Jews, but I think others have a right to do that. I think the Blacks would prefer to be with their own kind, and there would be a lot of opposition here."

Finally, Mrs. Carnes implied that Blacks and Jews would be all right if they were enough like herself and others of her class, saying: "There does need to be compatibility, but I have no objection to Negro and Jewish members."

Racial and religious prejudice among upper-class women is evident from these comments. Blacks, Jews, and other "unacceptable" people are not welcome in upper-class clubs; and it is the function of invitational membership to keep them out.[4] More open membership is unacceptable, except to the few newcomers in this sample. And even newcomers choose selection methods, such as income, that exclude nearly everyone but people like themselves. Membership in upper-class clubs and associations is a catch-22: only the right people can belong; but unless they already belong, they are not the right people.

Certainly one function of the exclusivity of upper-class clubs is the exclusion of certain people from the class. Such clubs, however, must play a more personal, more positive, part in the lives of individual members. When asked what membership meant to them in personal terms, the women replied: "When it comes to clubs, I'm the worst snob you know. People have a right to choose their friends" (Mrs. Carpenter). "The function of the club is to be with friends. If you let every Tom, Dick and Harry in, it loses its point" (Mrs. Appleton).

They spoke repeatedly of the club as a place to meet and be with their friends. In a somewhat softer version of the statements made above, Mrs. Haines said: "We belong because our friends belong and it's a good way to see our friends." They added that the shared social background of club members enhanced friendships: "You want to have some place to go and see your friends and have everybody be congenial and from the same background" (Mrs. Haines). "Congeniality is important . . . people who like each other and are from similar backgrounds" (Mrs. Holt).

Mrs. Farley, admitting the negative nature of exclusivity, added that a shared sense of history and traditions is important to friendships: "Sometimes I think the exclusion of people is dreadful, but there's a place for it. I think there has to be some anchors of tradition, a few things that are a part of the past, a place where you can go and be with people you're comfortable with."

Another aspect of social clubs is their use for entertaining. Mrs. Hammond said that she and her husband entertain frequently at clubs. And Mrs. Carnes said: "[The club] is a big part of our lives. Most of our entertaining is done at the club, and most of our friends belong." Mrs. Carnes also hinted that the social clubs present suitable opportunities for class-compatible marriages, saying, "I met my husband there."

For other women, social clubs have little personal importance. They claim that they rarely go to the clubs and are unsure why they continue their costly memberships. For Mrs. Miles, belonging to an upper-class club is a matter of family tradition rather than individual satisfaction: "We belong to too many clubs. It's ridiculous, but it's a matter of having belonged all my life. We don't use them much."

Women for whom social clubs were of little personal importance explained their continued memberships in terms of the need to maintain networks and associations for "socializing" within the class. As Mrs. Lane said: "I've only been to [the club] once this year. I'm really a loner, but I feel I have to go and be pleasant even though I don't want to. Part of our way of life is that I should be sociable."

Mrs. Hoight expressed the view that while some of the women of her class genuinely enjoy belonging to clubs and attending club activities, others went because they felt they had to: "I think half the members go because they like it and half because they think it's a social necessity."

Mrs. Wright provided a more specific social-networking motivation for her continued membership in a local downtown club. Claiming that the club was useful for holding meetings and encouraging people to attend them, she said: "We don't feel we should withdraw our support even though we don't go much anymore. They're important for meetings. We get a better attendance when the Arts Board meets [at the club]."

These reasons for club membership go beyond the desire for exclusivity in personal friendships. They recognize the greater function of the clubs to build and maintain class traditions, networks, and associations. Many upper-class women, therefore, continue their membership in clubs even though they actively dislike them or gain little individual satisfaction from their memberships. Their comments sent me looking for a way to link the personal and social concerns of my subjects.

A few of the women talked about friendships that allow persons not born into the upper class to eventually become accepted into upper-class clubs and social circles. Mrs. Clarke said that, although she supported invitational memberships, she also believed that the membership should be "broadened to include anybody who seems appropriate." When I asked her how it would be decided who was appropriate and who was not, she replied: "By their friends and the world they live in. Most of the people who are members are friends before they become members. They like to do similar things in a similar way. I think that's important for a private club."

This seemed very similar to the process of "getting in" that many of the women talked about—a process which the newcomers in the sample had gone through. The process consisted of "becoming known" and of finding an already well-established member to "sponsor" their membership. Mrs. Holt explained that, "even with the new [more open] policy in the League, you have to be known to a number of people already in the League to be accepted."

Mrs. Carpenter, the current president of the local upper-class women's club, described how new people were accepted for membership following the process of becoming known and finding a sponsor: "We're full now. When people resign we take new members. We have a waiting list. Three [current] members have to write letters, and then we vote on each one. They have to be attractive, interested in civic things, art, music, friends of your friends and of your friends' friends."

Other women spoke of the importance of the right sponsors. Mrs. Miles said simply, "What matters is who you know and [whether] you are going to fit in." Mrs. Brownley remarked: "Who does the proposing [of new members for clubs] makes a big difference, what kind of people they are."

Mrs. Wainwright called attention to the importance of family members as sponsors and to the secrecy of the process: "My mother-in-law asked if I wanted to join, and then I was simply invited one day. It's done very secretly. I don't know how."

Mrs. Smythe spoke of her own sense of awkwardness when she was asked to sponsor someone whom she did not wish to sponsor: "It's hard if someone says to you they would like to belong, and you don't particularly want to put them up."

For people from out of town, sponsorship may occur through a letter of introduction from a member of an upper-class club in another city which is known to those considering the applicant for the local club. Mrs. Appleton described how this process was happening to someone currently being considered for membership in her club: "I know of someone who has just moved here. Her club sent a letter telling us she would be a valuable member. Several people have met her and think that would be a grand idea. I haven't met her yet." She intended to make up her own mind about the new woman, reserving her judgement until she met her. At the same time, it was clear that the woman would not even have been considered without the letter of introduction.

I asked Mrs. Appleton if the letter was a common format for persons of her social group moving to or from other cities. She responded not only with a useful comment about this particular strategy for "getting in," but also with a highly class-conscious description of the national upper-class network: "I'd say [the letter of introduction idea] is pretty typical, although we all know each other anyway, perhaps from boarding school or from having spent our summers together in Maine. I know people from all over. That's just the way it is. That's the kind of life this is. You just know people. I don't know any other kind of life, and it's nice."

Mrs. Appleton seemed to feel that she would know someone of the upper class from another city through the larger class network. Other women felt that the local upper-class organizations were more closed than that, requiring local ties for acceptance of new members. Mrs. VanHague said that, in order to become a member, an out-of-towner "would have to know someone in town." She acknowledged that "if you came here without knowing anyone, it could be very difficult. As your husband got business connections, they could help you, and a young woman would also know friends in the community from school."

Mrs. Bennett agreed with Mrs. VanHague, at least in terms of her own experience: "This city was a pretty tight little place when I grew up. We all knew each other, and didn't make any effort for people who came new. I had a close friend from another city once and she said it was three years before she was invited to someone's house."

Even Mrs. Brownley (who thought that an outsider might get in with the help of a letter and that she might be known from national upper-class resorts or schools) said: "I've only lived here a short time, twenty years. Most of [the others in the club] have lived in [the city] for two or three generations. I married into an old family, about six generations."

Mrs. Brownley was not really a "newcomer." She was, herself, of upper-class origins and New England stock; and two decades ago, she had married into one of the city's oldest and wealthiest families. The real "newcomers"—those not born into the upper class, women who were not from the city or whose husbands were not upper class by birth, but had achieved top positions in business—described the process from more personal experience. Mrs. Atherton explained how she and her husband had been admitted into the city's oldest, upper-class country club: "If you're a newcomer you have to be sponsored. The owners of my husband's firm are a well-known family in the city, so that was enough of a recommendation for us. They said he was a good candidate and the rest took it on faith. People can have a party for the purpose of looking you over. We're giving one soon for someone who's been proposed. To my knowledge, we've never been cased ourselves, but maybe I have been and I didn't know it."

Mrs. Atherton went on to say that, in spite of formal acceptance of herself and her husband into the club, she did not believe that the old families would ever accept them on equal terms: "Although we do belong to the most prestigious club, I do sometimes get the feeling that they're opened up to heads of firms, to affluent people, just to pay the bills."

Mrs. Brownley, who served frequently on club admissions committees, corroborated that view: "I know lots of members come in on business memberships where a company belongs and may pay the membership fee. The company chooses the man. I don't know if I should be talking to you about it, but I know it goes on."

Mrs. Nesbitt, also a "newcomer," described the path of acceptance for herself and her husband as follows: "The word goes out. Some of my husband's firm's board members invited us to dinner, and they said we should join these clubs. But this didn't happen until four months after we'd moved here."

Even if one gets through the process of becoming known and finding a sponsor, Mrs. Hughes points out that there are still more hurdles to finally being accepted as a member: "[The upper class country club] is always full. You have to practically wait for somebody to die [to join]. You have to know a good percentage of the membership to get in, and it's very expensive."

The path to membership in upper-class social clubs, then, consists of a process of becoming known to the established upper class, and being sponsored by a member of this class for acceptance into the clubs. This process occurs primarily through the class-exclusive networks of personal friendships that develop among members of the upper class.

Summary and Conclusion

The women interviewed for this study generally agree that the central feature of upper-class clubs is exclusivity, which is maintained by invitational membership. Exclusivity restricts members to those defined as "congenial" or "compatible," and as "nice people." This definition inevitably means that people with different values, interests or ways of life—people from backgrounds other than the established upper class—are considered unacceptable. Blacks and Jews are almost automatically excluded. The women explain away their prejudices and acts of discrimination by suggesting, for example, that Blacks and Jews themselves discriminate in their own social organizations; and, they would be willing to accept people of different races and religions if these people were more like themselves.

In personal terms, the clubs provide most women with places to be with friends—people of similar backgrounds and traditions. Other women get little personal satisfaction out of their club memberships, though they continue to belong. These women note that the social functions and social imperatives of upper-class clubs provide important networks and associational patterns within the class.

Personal friendships are sometimes a way to get into upper-class clubs, providing a link between the personal and social importance of the clubs. In order to be accepted, one must "become known" and be "sponsored" by a member. One accomplishes this primarily through networks of personal friendships; and the participation in such networks and the "sponsoring" process is an expected part of upper-class life. This process, as the final chapter discusses, is sometimes in tension with the personal friendships from which it emerges.

This discussion is somewhat circular, which is, indeed, the point. Membership in upper-class clubs is limited primarily to persons already of the upper class. A small number of persons who are not to the manner born[5] may eventually become enough like them in their way of life and patterns of association to be accepted. Upper-class clubs are thus a primary mechanism by which members control access to their class. This process ensures that the upper class does not become merely a social caste with access limited to birthright, since the process does allow for the gradual absorption into the social networks and organizations of the class a few carefully selected "new" persons of wealth, status, and power.[6] But the process also ensures that the new people, those not born into the class, share the values, outlook, and general way of life of the class. This insulates the class from fundamental change; but it protects the class from complete stagnation, which might seriously weaken its positon.

Upper-class social clubs—and the women in them—create and maintain a social fabric for upper-class life. The consequent class cohesion and solidarity[7] construct an organizational and cultural base for the exercise of authority and power in the community.[8] The next chapter will explore one way upper-class women use this power in the community—serving, in a voluntary capacity, on the boards of major cultural, educational, and charitable institutions of the city.

Community
Volunteer

6

"It's offered me a way of life that I find very satisfactory. My mother was very prominent, very active in all sorts of activities, so I was raised in this tradition of public service, serving on committees and boards of schools, hospitals and agencies. My grandparents were involved as well. This was just how you spent your time. You didn't just read or play bridge. You saw what community needs were and you pitched in to do something about them. After college I joined the Junior League and had a very intensive training in community problems. My generation had help in the home when we were raising our children so we had time. Also I've never had the necessity of earning my own living, so I haven't had to take a paid job. I don't know what I would have done with my life without this. I've been very lucky to do volunteer work."

Mrs. Eton offers a typical description of community volunteer work in the lives of upper-class women: it is personally satisfying; it is a family tradition; it is a way to contribute to the community; it is entered through exclusive class networks like the Junior League; and it is possible because of their economic position. In short, it is a way of life.

All of the women I interviewed were involved in some sort of community work, though the amount of time and numbers of organizations served varied considerably. The most active women served on four or five boards of the city's major cultural institutions (such as the art museum and the symphony orchestra), colleges and universities, health organizations (especially clinics and hospitals), and social welfare and other charitable organizations (for example, child and family welfare agencies, and the United Way). They often took turns chairing various boards; and many of them had received some formal recognition for their work in the form of award plaques, which they proudly displayed to me. The less active volunteers, a distinct minority, often served on membership committees of organizations like the Garden Center, the Health Museum, and the Playhouse; or they participated in annual fundraising events for their college, garden club, or a particular charity. Several of these women had been more active volunteers earlier in their lives.[1]

Upper-class women are not, for the most part, involved in direct service kinds of volunteer work. They do not, for example, push a flower cart in the hospital; answer telephones at the school or library; staff the entry desk at the museum; or comfort sick, abused, or neglected children and adults. The few women who had done direct service activities had performed them early in their volunteer careers, for a relatively short period of time.

Instead, upper-class women move quickly into leadership positions on the boards of their organizations. From these positions, they influence organizational operations and policy, and carry out what they perceive as their primary task—fundraising. They perform this task well because—according to their own explanations—of their monied connections in the community, their direct links to the people and groups who have money to contribute and who know how to mobilize others to contribute. The combination of skilled leadership and social and monied connections is institutionalized through that organizational prototype of upper-class volunteerism—the Junior League.

The Junior League, founded in New York in 1901, is a national service organization for women volunteers. Membership is by invitation only; and the membership criteria, in terms of both social background and the amount of work expected, are stringent ones. Although membership is, in and of itself, no longer sufficient to designate one a member of the upper class (the League now admits carefully chosen upper-middle-class women), it is historically and traditionally an upper-class organization.[2]

All but three of the women I interviewed for this study had belonged to the Junior League at some time. The women who had never belonged felt it necessary to "explain" this non-normative behavior. Mrs. Wright, for example, had grown up in a small town where there was no Junior League affiliate. Mrs. Nesbitt, a "newcomer" who had more liberal views than many of the women, said: "I was asked to join the Junior League, but I didn't want to because I figured if you wanted to do volunteer work you didn't need to join a special group to do it. I didn't need it for my ego, and I think some people do."

For most, the League is part of the "way of life" of volunteerism described by Mrs. Eton at the beginning of this chapter. Mrs. Wainwright explained, "Volunteerism is crucial [to understanding our way of life], and the Junior League is the quintessence of volunteer work."

The League operates as a training ground for young women on their way up to board positions. During a probationary period that socializes them to dedicated service, careful tabulations are kept of the hours they serve before they are accepted into full League membership. The League offers courses to familiarize the women with community problems and issues and to provide them with leadership skills. As Mrs. Holt said: "The orientation courses are very good. You quickly become acquainted with the community and are exposed to experts in their fields."

The finished product is a skilled and reliable volunteer. Mrs. Hughes, a woman from one of the oldest and wealthiest family backgrounds, said: "The Junior League has well-trained, responsible volunteers who are trained to be leaders. The admission standards are tough, not in terms of breeding, but in terms of ability." Mrs. Chambers described League members as "well-educated, conscientious volunteers with pretty much the same background. You expect them to do a good job."

In addition to providing valuable leadership skills, the Junior League—like all upper-class volunteer organizations—provides its members with a class-exclusive social network. "The League is congenial, selective, and you have to be known to a number of people in the League to be accepted" (Mrs. Holt). Mrs. Chambers pointed out that, in her view, the League "would cease to be the League if it were not invitational. We're a group of women with our own social background, educated, with a tradition of service," she said. Mrs. Harper, putting it somewhat more bluntly but not at all critically, said, "There is a certain amount of snob appeal."

The women recognized that the exclusivity of the League contributes to the building of class networks that operate collectively in the community. Mrs. Chambers said: "The League is composed of people who work together well and instinctively understand each other because of their common background. We're cohesive and we stand together."

This aspect of the League is especially important to women from other cities. Mrs. Hoight said, "You can move to another town and find other Junior Leaguers just like you." She also noted the importance of learning about the community through the League: "It's a great advantage especially for people moving here from another city, because you immediately are exposed to the community in a way that might otherwise take a much longer time."

The women were also well aware that the social exclusivity of the League enhances its economic and political weight. Mrs. Smythe, a dynamic woman known for her ability to mobilize financial backing for downtown renewal projects, said, "If you belong to the League, doors open for you." Mrs. Clarke claimed, "Without the League, I might not have been able to get to the board level." And Mrs. Garson, a veteran volunteer approaching her eighth decade, agreed, saying that "there are volunteer organizations that will take volunteers of any type, but these other volunteers don't have the power and financial backing that the League does."

Finally, the League (and upper-class volunteerism in general) is not intended to bring about fundamental social change or reform. Indeed, many of the women do not believe that social reform as a solution to community problems is possible (as this chapter later shows). But it is only practical to help some individuals improve their own lives. Volunteerism, therefore, provides community services and improvements that may make things better for the few who have access to them.

Mrs. Wainwright spoke of this feature of the League's activities when she said: "Everything the League does improves the situation but it doesn't rock the boat. It fits into existing institutions."

This is a general description of the community volunteer work of upper-class women and of the primary organization through which such activity is institutionalized, the Junior League. I next asked the women about their volunteer work in terms of personal motivations and gratification.

Personal Views of Volunteer Work and Paid Work

Mrs. Hoight is well known in the community for her work in charitable activities. Typically, she enjoys the opportunity presented by volunteerism to be involved at the top: "You can get higher in volunteerism than you would be able to as a paid employee. You can direct procedures and policy and get involved in the power structure." Mrs. Vincent "prefer[s] things where you get involved in making decisions." Mrs. Martin "enjoy[s] the leadership aspect." And Mrs. Farley said, "[I like] to get something going and then move on to something else; and I usually get moved up the administrative level pretty quickly."

Mrs. Clarke spoke of her satisfaction in being involved at the top of an organization: "The board level is where the interesting things are happening and where the decisions are made. I don't want the little jobs." Mrs. Chambers likes the chance to be creative and to be in charge. As she put it: "I get into creative jobs where I'm running the show myself."

For these upper-class women, on a personal level, volunteer work means being involved in organizations at the level of policy-making. It means being the leaders they were trained to be in the Junior League. It means taking a task from its early stages to completion and then moving on to something else. Paid professionals might give the same answers when asked about sources of job satisfaction. If the same kind of satisfaction is important to upper-class women volunteers, why, then, don't more of them pursue paid professional work?[3]

There is some sense among upper-class women that volunteer work is "better" than paid work—and that volunteers are better workers:

"A volunteer is someone who's been brought up to give of her time, someone who's dedicated . . . I think there's a big difference in work attitudes between volunteer workers and paid workers. The paid workers stop working at a certain time and won't lift a finger after that. The volunteer will work all night if we have a project we have to get done. That comes from education and commitment. Maybe that's where family background comes in. We've been brought up ← Snobbish to do more than is expected of us. There are many people who won't lift a finger to help. They'll take their forty-five minutes for lunch no matter what's happening." (Mrs. Harper)

This comment suggests a clear sense of class superiority, a belief that volunteer workers are somehow "better" than those who receive a salary. Mrs. Appleton also reflected this feeling of superiority when she said, "We do it because we want to, so we do a better job than people who work because they need the money."

Mrs. Haines agreed, saying: "It's not like a nine to five job. It's with you constantly. If a job doesn't get done, you end up doing it yourself." She did recognize that not everyone has the luxury of doing the kind of job she is able to do, and she added that "You have to be able to afford the luxury of being a volunteer. It's an expensive proposition, both moneywise and timewise."

Mrs. Haines, Mrs. Appleton and Mrs. Vincent added another dimension to the theme of class superiority: they saw volunteer work as a mark of privilege. Mrs. Haines said, "If you're born like we are, you don't have to work." Mrs. Appleton agreed, saying, "If you don't need the money, you shouldn't be greedy." And Mrs. Vincent added: "I did volunteer work because I didn't need to make a living. It could be considered a luxury."

Volunteer work allows these upper-class women to see themselves as someone "better" than people who do paid work. It sets them off from people who depend on salaries; and it maintains an important social distinction between themselves and those whom they see as very different from themselves.

117

Mrs. Haines, however, spoke for a number of women when she said that she lacks the formal educational and occupational experience to obtain the kind of paid work she would want to do. "I don't know what I'm qualified to do," she said, "I'm not really qualified for anything." Mrs. Smythe made a similar comment, saying, "If I went into paid work, I would have to put up with a job too menial for me." Mrs. Appleton agreed, recognizing that she had "never been trained to do anything." And Mrs. Harper said, "I'd like to get more involved in education, but I don't have the professional training."

Having not acquired the formal credentials to do paid professional work, these women know that they can get farther using their class position, their family names, and the informal training they received in the Junior League and on the boards. Volunteerism is, indeed, a better arena than paid work for getting the kinds of work they want to do, and for getting into decision-making and leadership positions.

For many of the women, home and family responsibilities are another reason they prefer volunteer to paid work. Mrs. Lane said, "I travel a lot with my husband, so I can't take on a continuous job." Mrs. Farley explained: "Volunteer work is more flexible time-wise. You can fit in family responsibilities. If I hadn't gotten married, I probably would have worked." Like Mrs. Farley, many women cited their activities as wives and mothers as reasons for preferring volunteer work to paid work. They felt that it would be very difficult to carry on these essential activities and meet the structured demands of salaried jobs.

The women's comments about home and family responsibilities being obstacles to paid work were, again (like their comments about being wives and mothers), strikingly similar to those of women of other classes. For example, Mrs. Langdon said: "If I had a job, there would be set hours. What would I do with a sick child? I wouldn't take a full-time job now."

Mrs. Garson added: "I don't think I could take a job and

run a family. I don't have the energy. I tried to go back to work after my children were grown, but I would have had to take a whole lot of courses to catch up. . . . And I was so involved in the community and my husband needed my support in his work. I always thought I would go back to school, but I never did."

Mrs. Clarke agreed: "I think two demanding jobs . . . a husband and a household with three children . . . would just be too much. And by taking this time out to have a family . . . fifteen years . . . you've lost that time from a career, so your chances of performing at peak level in your fifties and sixties are less."

For the most part, the women seemed satisfied with their balance of home, family, and volunteer work. Home and family responsibilities, therefore, are incentives to volunteer work rather than obstacles to paid work. According to Mrs. Harper: "Volunteers don't want a paid job. Their husbands are successful and work lots of evenings, and somebody's got to be home to keep things going."

Mrs. Appleton pointed out that if she had a paid job, "there wouldn't be any leisure." Mrs. Miles agreed, saying: "I've never really thought about a paid job. I have four children and a husband who's active in many civic things. We like to take long vacations in the winter, and we have children coming home to visit from college and that sort of thing. I couldn't do all that if I had a job."

Mrs. Haines made similar remarks: "There are few jobs that would have left me free to run the house and go off on trips and do things with the children. If my husband has two weeks vacation, I can just stop the volunteer work."

Mrs. VanHague's comments seemed to challenge earlier statements about volunteers being more dedicated and hard-working than paid workers. She said: "What's nice about being a volunteer is that you can always say that you're going out of town, and they get a substitute. And since you're not getting paid, they can't say very much to you about it."

I also thought that the women's volunteer work might enhance their husbands' occupational success or social standing in the community, in ways that paid work could not. This appeared, for the most part, *not* to be the case. In response to an open question about how they helped their husbands' careers, most women mentioned activities such as those discussed in Chapter 3. Only a few newcomers mentioned their volunteer work. Mrs. Atherton, for example, said: "I know my volunteer work enhances my husband's position. Let's say the wife of a client of ours asked me to serve on a committee. If I accept it, it makes her think well not only of me but of my husband as well. I think it has a very real connection to your husband's position in the community."

Mrs. Wright, whose own family is an old established one, had married a Jew who was not accepted by them. She said: "I think some of the contacts I have [through my volunteer work] have helped him to be known. . . . It was just a matter of introducing him and then he made his own way."

The volunteer activities of these less-established women might, therefore, be helpful to their husbands. But most of the women from old, well-known and influential families, married to men from the same class, do not think their volunteer work is helpful to their husbands. Mrs. Howe said, "That's never occurred to me. He stands on his own." Mrs. Brownley recognized that some women do such work to help their husbands, but that she did not have to do so.

Some women were critical of those who do volunteer work for such reasons. Mrs. Haines said: "I think there are a lot of girls who do volunteer work for the wrong reasons. Say your husband needs more clients, or you're new in town. The only way they're going to make it is to get out and around. These husbands want their wives visible in the community. They love it when their wives are on the social page. People do it to get ahead socially. They decide they want to be fancy, and the easiest way to get to be fancy is to get to work on a volunteer job with fancy people."

There is further indication that community work is not seen as a substantial support to the husband's position: several of the husbands were actually opposed to their wives' volunteer activities. This opposition was usually directed toward wives who had achieved particularly high positions in their work. Mrs. Carpenter, for example, said of her husband: "He's been negative about what I wanted to do. He's opposed to my being chairman of the board. It's an affront to his manhood. He doesn't mind if I sit at the reception desk at the museum, and he'd love it if I played bridge. He has the idea that a woman's place is in the home making the man happy."

Mrs. Hoight spoke similarly of her husband's attitude: "He's really jealous of all this outside stuff I do. He doesn't like it, and he won't come to a meeting I'm conducting. He'd like me to stay home more than I do and be more supportive."

It appears that the community volunteer work done by these upper-class women, like business entertaining, is not a significant support to their husbands' position. This is not to say that it plays absolutely no role in this respect. Mrs. Brownley said that, although her husband did not need her help, it "certainly hasn't done him any harm that people know I'm interested in the community." Nevertheless, except for women who are newcomers or otherwise not completely accepted into upper-class circles, such activity does not seem to directly enhance or uphold the position of men in the economic or social structure.

There are, then, several advantages to volunteer work: it allows the women to obtain leadership positions that they might not be able to achieve as paid workers; it allows them to maintain class distinctions between themselves and those who are dependent on paid work; and, it allows them to continue the home and family responsibilities and general way of life that they enjoy. As with their activities as wives and mothers, however, there is a certain level of dissatisfaction with volunteer activities. In both cases, it appears that the women's movement has had some impact on upper-class women.

Tensions in Volunteerism

When I asked what they would do differently if they had their lives to live over again, many of the women responded to this open question in terms of work. Mrs. Wainwright, for example, said: "If I had it to do over again, I'd definitely train for a profession. But there was no pressure to do that and I was hell-bent for marriage. My father actually said to me, 'You don't ever have to work. We'd be very happy just to have you stay home, as a matter of fact, we'd prefer it.' Then I saw the alternative of volunteer work, but I feel very strongly about being paid and the responsibility you're given. I get the jobs that are left over."

Nearly half of the thirty-six women expressed the wish that they had obtained more "practical" educations or paid jobs prior to marriage. Mrs. Hoight said, "If I had worked as hard as a professional for the past twenty years as I have as a volunteer, I probably would be the head of an agency now, and I probably would have made a greater contribution." In a strikingly parallel comment, Mrs. Carpenter said; "If I'd used my energies in paid work, I probably could have been head of a corporation."

Mrs. Hall had said she thought her early years in volunteer work were wasted and wanted, over her husband's objections, to pursue a career in science. She spoke with anger about how she had been led to where she is now:

> "I was never given the opportunity to go to college. My older sister went so far as to take the college boards and was accepted at Radcliffe and then was told she could not go. Women, according to my parents, were not supposed to go to college. We were both sent to a French school for girls in New York where we learned art appreciation, were taken to symphonies and operas, and taught how to be perfect young ladies. We were given aptitude tests at [school] and later I learned that I had done the best in the school in science. My

mother knew this, but I was not encouraged to puruse a course in science because that was not for a woman. Now my interest in science has become a serious one, and I've taken some courses . . . but I know I'll never finish."

"If I had it to do over," Mrs. Hall said, "I'd have majored in something different in college, something I could do now. I wish before we'd had any children that I'd had a paid job. It's important to train yourself for something, to pursue something in depth."

In fact, about a third of the women interviewed were somewhat reluctant volunteers. Though they had not withdrawn from volunteer work (as Mrs. Wainwright, Mrs. Hall, and Mrs. Ames had done), they did express generally negative views about it. Eight of these women expressed a clear preference for paid work, suggesting that they would be taken more seriously as paid professionals.

Mrs. Spears, the only full-time paid professional in the sample, corroborated these views. She felt that her occupation made a significant difference in what she was able to accomplish on the boards as a volunteer. She said, "On an awful lot of boards, the women turn the crank and the men make the real decisions. Now that I'm a paid professional and I'm asked to serve on boards, I'm not asked to do the kind of secretarial work some of the other women do, like getting out mailings. I'm taken seriously now." Mrs. Carnes, who had recently taken a temporary part-time job, concurred with Mrs. Spears: "My [paid part-time] job is more challenging than being on women's committees or getting into one thing after another with no real depth."

These experiences are reflected in other studies of boards of community organizations. Ratcliff, Gallagher, and Ratcliff, for example, found in their study in St. Louis that, although upper-class women participate extensively on the boards of civic organizations, evidence suggested that upper-class men dominate those organizations. Tickamyer also found that wealthy men are dominant and wealthy women's participation in charitable organizations is no higher than men's.[5] Male dominance on community boards may explain some of the women's dissatisfaction.

In spite of their dissatisfaction, however, few women were making any concrete moves to change their work opportunities. For some, like Mrs. Hall and Mrs. Wainwright, it may too late; but for most, the pursuit of paid work requires giving up too much of an enjoyable lifestyle. As Mrs. Clarke said, "I don't want to give up the quality of life we're able to have because I'm [at home]. I don't think I could be a career woman with a demanding job." Thus, even when the women are dissatisfied in their volunteer activities—or their activities as wives—and might benefit from changes, their upper-class way of life wins out.

Other tensions arise from community activities, which have to do with the actual value of the work itself. Most of the women derive personal satisfaction and a feeling of accomplishment from the work they do. At the same time, the value of these accomplishments is somewhat vague, from the point of actually solving community problems.

The volunteer work of upper-class women has an elusive quality about it, and specific accomplishments, in terms of actually improving the life of the community, are difficult to come by. Mrs. Holt is a dedicated and influential community activist. In what appeared to be a slip of the tongue accompanied by a flush of apparent embarrassment, she said, "It's that illusion of being useful that's satisfying." Mrs. Smythe referred to volunteer work as "a demonstration of sincerity." And Mrs. Harper confessed, "I'm not sure that what I've done has really accomplished anything, a lot of it is busy work."

Mrs. Haines is active as a volunteer in cultural and arts organizations, rather than charitable and social service ones. She described the experience that led her to stop charitable work, suggesting that it accomplished little and was demeaning to both giver and recipient: "I can remember when I was working with the [Junior] League and I had to go into the inner city in a really terrible neighborhood . . . to teach girls to sew. We would take off our engagement rings . . . and wear our simplest clothes . . . you felt like a fraud. I found they would have preferred that I give them the fifteen dollars I was paying the cleaning woman to watch [my] children while I went off to do my lady bountiful act. . . . I'd rather give them the fifteen dollars."

Mrs. Wainwright, Mrs. Hall and Mrs. Ames, had largely given up volunteer work because they felt its accomplishments were not substantial enough. Mrs. Wainwright, speaking of the United Way, said that it "isn't intended to solve problems." Mrs. Hall offered that she had quit the Junior League because it seemed to her that "the most important thing was how neat your hat was." Mrs. Ames said, "I think they should stop being so involved in the embellishing and beautifying and get to some of the real problems . . . like crime and drugs and all the masses of people."

Mrs. Sharpe, who is very enthusiastic about volunteerism, is most interested in the serious racial and economic problems in the city. When I asked her what she thought her work contributed to the community, she said: "Anything we do is just a drop in the bucket. I really don't see any solution. Welfare is inadequate and the less money there is, the less education and then no jobs."

She then went on to describe something she had done that seemed useful to her:

> "I do find it personally gratifying when I can help people that really need it, when there's a crisis and there just isn't anybody else. A family in the inner city area where our agency is, had a house burned several years ago. The father didn't have a job, and I guess he wasn't well, but mostly he was drunk. We did everything we could for the mother . . .

a little bit of furniture to start again, some cooking utensils, some clothes. I gave her a couple of hundred dollars a year, and she wouldn't even be able to put clothes on the children's back if it weren't for outside help. She's a worthwhile person trying to bring up a family as well as she can. One son is really quite bright, but he's always getting into trouble in school. So, I talked to his counselor . . . they're Black, of course . . . and got him enrolled in a boarding school [out of state]. He's away from the father there, and I think he'll do a lot better. The last time I sent the mother a check, she was so grateful. She only manages to get along with this little help from me."

Since Mrs. Sharpe did not think that anything she or others like her could do was a real solution—that it was "just a drop in the bucket"— what did she think of a governmental solution to poverty, such as a guaranteed income? She answered: "I don't see how you can have a guaranteed annual income for people who just won't work. The ones who work are just going to be supporting the ones who don't work. I think education is fundamental to what they need. Instead of spending money on jobs they can't keep, they should spend it for training, like trade school."

Asked what she thought about the option of college for poor Black youth, she said: "That's fine if they're able to do it, but so many of them get scholarships and they last a year and then they flunk out. I'm not very optimistic about that until they get better backgrounds, get better prepared for college."

Mrs. Sharpe described two other occasions when she felt she had been helpful on a small scale. One was a personal effort: "Every summer I get about eighty kids from the [city's black ghetto] and bring them out for a day at my place in the country."

Her other effort was made through the private social welfare organization which was founded by and named for her family. This agency, on whose board she serves, is located in a poor black neighborhood:

> "One year [the board] decided to try to do something so the people would care more about the appearance of their neighborhood. So we gave them all windowboxes and said we would give a prize to the family who had the best one. It was really lots of fun. They didn't know anything about growing windowboxes, but I think it really did help them to take an interest in the neighborhood's appearance. We also open the [agency] so they can have meetings there if they wish. We have a family day when everyone comes, and a Christmas with Santa Claus and presents. So, I think the [agency] stands for something in that community, and I think the people there are proud of it."

Mrs. Sharpe described another volunteer project that she had been involved with which was a failure because the neighborhood essentially refused it:

> "It really was very unfortunate when my garden club did the grounds of [an historic house in the inner city]. We did it just like it would have been originally, a vegetable garden, grape arbor, apple orchard. The very first night they planted those apple trees, the neighborhood kids came in and sawed down every single tree. When we went around and asked the people in the neighborhood what they thought about that, they said that the children had always played there. We said there was a playground two blocks away, but they said why shouldn't the children play right where they always had. Well, that really stopped any effort on the part of our garden club to improve that area."

Like Mrs. Sharpe, most of the women were at a loss to say exactly how the considerable time, energy, and money that they put into community volunteer work actually helps the community. They were more likely to agree with Mrs. Sharpe and Mrs. Smythe that "some things are never going to be solved." This was true of both the two-thirds of the sample who were very positive and enthusiastic about their volunteer work, and the one-third that was reluctantly involved. Why did they work so hard at these activities, if they were not sure that they were actually solving community problems and addressing community needs?

Carrying On The Class

Mrs. Carpenter told a short story that provided a clue. She said: "[I learned the importance of volunteer work when] every Christmas we were made to choose our favorite new toy, and our parents took us out, and we gave it to a poor family. They wanted us to see what is was like not to have any new toys."

Similarly, Mrs. Hall finds volunteer work a necessary, if empty, gesture compared with her "debt to society." Pointing to the expansive view of the valley seen from her outdoor patio, she said: "I feel enormous guilt sitting up here with all this, when so many people don't have it. It has inspired me to want to prove to people that those born with the luck of money are not all bastards, that some of us are worthwhile people."

Indeed, the most common reason given by the women for their volunteer work is a sense of social obligation. They do volunteer work to "pay off" what they see to be their debt to society, to try to justify and legitimate their class privilege. They spoke with resounding sameness:

> "I think that if you are blessed, then you should turn around and do your share." (Mrs. Hammond)

> "I feel we owe something to society. I was grateful for what I had, and I wanted to give something." (Mrs. Hughes)

"I was brought up by my family that the more you have the more is your responsibility to your fellow man." (Mrs. Ames)

"To whom much is given, much is expected." (Mrs. Smythe)

"When you have more than your share, you should return what you can to the community." (Mrs. Brownley)

This "noblesse oblige" reflects the extent to which class is used as a context to make sense of volunteerism. Their volunteer work, as they themselves define it, justifies their existence as members of the privileged class. It staves off the charges (such as those discussed in the second chapter) that their privileges are unearned and undeserved.

Since the work has a class purpose beyond solving problems or addressing needs, it does not need to contribute to the community in a major way. For the purpose of the class, it need only be "a demonstration of sincerity," "an illusion of being useful." This is not to suggest that such work never does actually improve the community; but improvement is not the only goal of the work for many of the upper-class women who engage in it. This is also not to suggest that such work is unimportant; indeed, it is essential to upholding the power and privilege of the upper class.

The upper-class tradition of service and sense of social responsibility, or noblesse oblige, as a means of justifying privilege is carried on through the family. It therefore becomes a family tradition, as well as a class tradition, and is perpetuated in this way. The women spoke of family tradition, again, with resounding sameness. This indicated to me the strong collective nature of their personal reality and the power of class as the fundamental framework within which they define their lives:

"I did the things my grandmother and my mother did, so it was a tradition and that was good." (Mrs. Martin)

"My grandfather was a member of the original board." (Mrs. Eton)

"I'm a responsible board member. You don't learn it. You're born with it." (Mrs. Hughes)

"I had the example of a family tradition of service." (Mrs. Chambers)

"My father-in-law is chairman of the board." (Mrs. Haines)

"Since I married into a prominent family, it was natural that I would get involved in the community." (Mrs. Brownley)

"I've taken mother's position on the board because she asked. The family has been involved in it for generations." (Mrs. Wilson)

"My family had been on the board, so it was natural that I would." (Mrs. Miles)

These responses have an "of course" quality about them which indicates that the women have little choice about their involvement in volunteer work. Mrs. Hughes spoke of it as something you're "born with", and Mrs. Miles said that it's just "natural." Mrs. Sharpe said: "If you're brought up this way, you just do it. You can't imagine not doing it." And Mrs. Wright stated that it's "just done, it's not talked about."

Volunteerism is, thus, an unquestioned activity for these upper-class women. It is a social form created by earlier generations, which is simply assumed and passed on to the next generation. But why is it so important? What, in addition to justifying class privilege and maintaining family tradition, is its ultimate goal? And what would be missing from the community and from society if there were no volunteers? The women answered this last question specifically in terms of class power.

"After all, the people who contribute most of the funds feel they deserve to have the major say about what's done with their money. The social workers in these agencies need someone to keep an eye on them." (Mrs. Wilson)

Mrs. Wilson and several other women interviewed feel that their jobs on various boards are, to some extent, necessary to maintain final authority over the paid professionals. As board members, they define policy for their organizations and, thus, direct the work of the paid staff. Mrs. Eton, for example, said, "You need people to give directions to the programs that employ the paid people."

In general, the women believe that they have a perspective on the organizations and the community that is in some way broader and therefore better than that of paid professionals. As Mrs. Holt put it: "You can't just rely on the professional to solve community problems. You need a broader perspective. The volunteer interprets to the community."

Mrs. Garson made the same point using the same terms. Mrs. Vincent, too, said, "Volunteers have a broader perspective than professionals." Mrs. Howe elaborated on this point, suggesting that the perspective of paid people is bounded by their particular discipline: "I bring to bear the perspective of the total community, where a particular agency fits in the broad scheme of things. I'm not blinded by any professional bias."

Mrs. VanHague suggested that the volunteer's broader perspective is the result of having more knowledge of the whole community. She said: "Many of the paid people don't know the city the way the volunteers do. I don't think they make as good judgments."

So even though volunteer work does not seem to solve community problems in substantive ways, it is important to directing policy and exercising control over the paid professionals in the organizations on whose boards they serve.

The women then spoke of client or consumer representation on the boards. They generally agree that "Clients tend to want to throw away what's being done and put the money somewhere else" (Mrs. Miles). They are opposed to such representation. They feel that clients do not understand what boards are supposed to do, and they do not make useful contributions. (This often means that clients disagree with the board about what should be done, and they are not very polite about it.) In addition to keeping tabs on paid professionals, then, another important task for upper-class board members is to check on clients and consumers. This is, at least in part, because they represent a challenge to the status quo that the women wish to maintain.

Moreover, there is clearly a political agenda in volunteer work. "I think it's important to keep things on an even keel so that things don't go too far over to the left," said Mrs. Hughes. "I think our job is to keep private institutions alive. One of the things you have to be careful of is too much government interference. I think you have more freedom with private money."

These upper-class women feel that they are protecting the "American way." They consider this an extremely important part of their task. They firmly believe that governmental institutions are a threat to liberty; and they equate an expanded role for the public sector or dependence on public money with socialism, communism, or a menace to democracy. Mrs. Ames, for example, said: "There must always be people to do volunteer work. If you have a society where no one is willing, then you may as well have communism where it's all done by the government."

Mrs. Hammond said, "I would be so opposed to a socialistic type of control. . . . The less the government is involved the better." Mrs. Holt concurred, saying that "if there were no volunteers, we would live in a completely managed society which is quite the opposite to our history of freedom."

Mrs. Holt expressed the generally shared view that private money is somehow less constrained than public money: "Private contributions are necessary in a democracy. It has a freer hand than public money." At the heart of volunteerism and the role of private money in protecting the "American way" is the issue of private control, or private power. Mrs. Hughes addressed this issue as an aspect of the freedom, or independence, the women spoke of. She said, "The more we can keep independent and under private control, the better it is."

What "private control" do my subjects believe they exercise to protect "democracy"? What notion of democracy is this? In exercising this control, which constituency do they believe they represent? And what, in their view, is the base of their power?

When I asked the women whom they represent on the boards, they spoke first of "the community." Mrs. Wright said, for example, "I represent the citizens at large." Mrs. Langdon said, "I think I'm just an interested member of the community." Initially, I accepted that to mean that they represent the general public, the people who live in the city served by their boards' art museums, universities, hospitals, and social agencies. Eventually, I questioned this, based on the distinction that my subjects made between client and consumer representation, between the "community" (by which they seemed to mean persons like themselves) and the "neighborhood" (by which they seemed to mean the broader community, a more heterogeneous representation of various classes, races, and ethnic groups).

When I asked more specifically which segment of the community they represent, the women most often answered (in terms similar to those in Chapter 2) with some description of the meaning of upper class. Mrs. Hughes, for example, said: "I do represent a certain part of the community. What do you call us? The old families, the traditionals, the real minority in this society, the people who have something. I represent that minority." Mrs. Howe agreed, saying of her position on the symphony board, "I represent an old-line family."

The "community," then, is apparently their own class. Mrs.

Langdon called attention to the fact that this class-based representation occurs partly as a consequence of class-based social networks. "I'd like to represent the community at large," she said, "but of course I can't know the thinking of people I'm not in contact with."

Private control was described as a more "democratic" alternative to funding and decision-making by government—even though private control is dominated by the upper class. As such, it is not democratic in the sense of representing various classes and racial and ethnic groups. Only one of the women, Mrs. Howe, seemed to have a sense of this. Describing herself as "terribly equalitarian," she told of her unsuccessful efforts to get the city's symphony orchestra board to broaden its base of representation: "As far as the board of trustees is concerned, I despair. They still have no Black members on the board. They have no musicians. There is much that must be done to bring that board into the twentieth century."

Mrs. Howe is not typical. Most of the women do not question the fact that their own class is significantly overrepresented on community boards. Nor do they question the fact that their overrepresentation is based in exclusive social networks of the sort described in the previous chapter on upper-class clubs. More importantly, it is the money itself, within these networks, that enables upper-class women to hold their positions on the boards. The money obtained through fundraising is a major source of private power.

Fundraising is the main task performed by virtually all of the women who serve as board members. Mrs. Haines asserted that "fundraising is absolutely at the top . . . the main thing that organizations want from you." All of the women recognize that they are valuable fundraisers because of their monied connections in the community. When I asked Mrs. Hughes, for example, what made her a good fundraiser, she said: "I know a lot of the people who are likely to give. I'm an entreé, I know the families of the people who have foundations . . . I've always known them."

Mrs. Lane made a similar statement about why she was asked to be on community boards: "We need the rich lady on our board to provide us with funds. . . . I'm one of the rich ladies. I don't bring a lot of know-how, but I'm getting good at fundraising and I like it. I've lived here all my life, and I probably know everybody I'm asking to contribute. I cross paths with them in both the business and the social community."

Like Mrs. Lane, Mrs. Holt believes that her work on community boards, her role in private control of community organizations, is possible because of her connections—primarily her connections to money. In a comment typical of many of the women, she said, "It's exceedingly important who asks whom for a gift. People do things for people as well as causes, and it's important to consider compatibility. It's helpful if you ask people to give money who know who you are. That's the advantage of being someone well known. You can't get anywhere if someone isn't [familiar with] your name. You have to have access to people and resources. It's a matter of living in the community over the years."

Mrs. Ames was also clear that her monied networks make her a valuable fundraiser. She spoke of the importance of reciprocity among people in the network: "If you do enough fundraising, it gets to the point that you scratch my back and I'll scratch yours. If they give to my project, I'll give to their's." Mrs. Smythe added that it is important to know who among one's friends in the network might give to a particular project: "You get to know who among your friends has a particular interest in what."

Some women include their husbands in the social network that enables them to raise funds for their organizations. That reference point, for them, creates a starting point for the exercise of power. Mrs. Atherton said, "I probably would not have gotten into those offices if my husband hadn't been where he is. If you want to get in to see the top man, you have to have clout, and I have it because my husband has done so many things for these people. I suppose each of the ones I approached owed him a favor."

Mrs. Haines spoke of the importance of her husband's family: "I think a lot of my qualifications for board work come from the fact that I've married a family name in [this city]. People will come to my home sometimes just to see the house, to get to know me and who I know—and then I think I have a talent for making people feel like they can contribute. It's like a business."

The women also presented their monied connections as their hold over paid staff and their leverage in discouraging client representation. Mrs. Eton—who earlier stated that board people should "give direction to the program that employ the paid people"—said that "somebody's got to go out and raise the money to pay the workers."

Mrs. Martin also believes that fundraising and managing the organizational budget are what make the volunteer "generalist" superior to the paid professional. "The generalist comes from the community, she said, and she can help the professional see what is possible in the general community—often, of course, in the field of funding." Mrs. Miles agreed, saying that "sometimes professionals don't understand what is financially feasible, or feasible in terms of the community."

In regard to client or consumer representation and the role of money in discouraging such representation, Mrs. Wright said: "I think it would be a matter of whether persons from these segments could reach money. Lawyers may refer a client who has funds to give, and bank executives also do this. Others from the community might not provide this service."

Mrs. Miles was quoted earlier as saying she opposed client representation because clients "tend to want to throw away what's being done and put the money somewhere else." She continued her comment, saying that "many [consumers] don't have a basic understanding of what it is a board is supposed to do. Perhaps this is due to financial limitations." Mrs. Clarke very succinctly stated that the role of people with monied connections on community boards is absolutely imperative. "I don't know how agencies would raise their budgets if it weren't for us, she said. "A lot of them would just disband."

Again, Mrs. Howe took a somewhat different view. She believes that private social service organizations, in particular, "wouldn't make it if they were to depend solely on the volunteer dollar." She believes that it is essential that current board members like herself work cooperatively with government rather than serving to minimize government involvement. She also believes that a broader base in terms of board membership is important to the financial circumstances of private cultural organizations. She said of her efforts to broaden the orchestra board, for example: "I thought that if the orchestra was going to survive, they were going to have to reach out and find new audiences. They couldn't survive if they were going to remain a closed corporation. . . . The present board has such tunnel vision as regards to their financial picture."

Mrs. Nesbitt also sees a major funding role for government. Speaking particularly of how private money is incapable of solving social problems, she said, "I favor solving all these problems with public funds through taxes." When asked if this would mean that she would pay considerably more in taxes, she responded with a goodnatured smile, "It certainly would."

Again, these comments are not typical; they serve primarily to cast the typical beliefs in bold relief. For the most part, these upper-class women believe that private funds are better than government funds, that their fundraising activities are essential to community organizations, and that such fundraising is the legitimate base of their own influence in these organizations. They are able to do fundraising because of their monied connections within the upper class; and their connections are clearly not available to members of other classes.

The consequence of their volunteer activities is the exercise of class power: power of volunteer boards over paid professionals, power to keep clients and consumers from gaining significant representation on community boards (which might result in their changing things), and power to maintain private, class control over institutions that might otherwise be run by the government. They exercise this power, as they themselves explained, as a result of their economic position in society. That is, they have monied connections in exclusive upper-class social networks; and they are able to contribute or withhold their own money as they see fit.

Summary and Conclusion

The evidence presented in this chapter demonstrates that volunteer work provides certain personal advantages to upper-class women (such as the opportunity to advance to leadership positions without formal credentials, and to balance home and family responsibilities). But these personal advantages do not explain their overall commitment to this work—especially since they describe volunteer work as "the illusion of being useful," and a "demonstration of sincerity" rather than a substantial contribution to solving community problems or addressing community needs. Instead, the women focus on class-specific reasons for doing volunteer work, such as noblesse oblige (which justifies privilege) and family tradition (which carries on the traditions of the class). These are the fundamental reasons for their commitment.

There are several consequences of upper-class volunteerism. The first is the justification of class privilege. The second is the creation and perpetuation of a social class network which, through its unique access to the economic resources of the society, can exercise private control over community organizations. This private control aims to set policy agenda that direct the paid staff; it also seeks to keep broader-based, non-upper class consumer or community input out of organizational decisions.

The idea of justifying class privilege means doing work in the community that shares, at some minimal level, the advantages of the upper class. It is primarily intended to mitigate charges that class privilege is unearned and undeserved. Such mitigation actually upholds the class by deflecting challenges to its privileged position in society. Because it legitimates the class, it maintains the position of the upper class in society. The creation of a class network— which exercises private control over community organizations— maintains the class itself in society.

This is the importance of the volunteer work done by upper-class women to the class structure. It upholds the upper class: it legitimates the class; it deflects challenges to its power; it constructs a class network that is inaccessible to people from other classes. That network derives from and contributes to the economic power of the upper class in society. Upper-class women would find no paid work that could begin to realize these ends.

Tensions
and
Contradictions

7

I have sought to demonstrate how upper-class women perform work that is necessary to maintain their class. Work is broadly defined here as activities that contribute in some way to the economic life of society. The work done by upper-class women is largely invisible: that is, it is unpaid and occurs outside the economic marketplace and labor force. Therefore, the women's role in creating and maintaining the economic and political power of the upper class is not typically recognized.

Preceding chapters have examined empirical evidence of consonance, stability, and the absence of change in the lives of upper-class women. This chapter asks what tensions and contradictions these women face and how they serve as forces for change. (Since the activities of upper-class women maintain their class, any significant *change* in their activities might constitute a potential change in the class structure.)

Tensions at the Personal Level

On the personal level, tensions are particularly evident in the role of the upper-class wife. A primary characteristic of the wifely activities described to me is a mode of accommodation: upper-class wives are expected to mold their lives to their husbands' lives. They should be available, for example, when the husbands want their wives to accompany them on business trips or to arrange social gatherings. In general, the women subjugate their own needs and scheduled activities to those of their husbands.

Like women of other classes, they are expected to take sole responsibility for running the household—though for upper-class women this does not typically mean doing housework, cooking, and shopping, but supervising the work done by others. Wives are also expected to serve as sounding boards when their husbands have troubles or triumphs to share from their work.

Like women of other classes, a number of these upper-class women expressed dissatisfaction with these expectations. They said, for example, that they do not like their husbands spending so much time at work away from home; and they object to their husbands' assumption that—women's scheduled activities being of little importance—the wives should always be available. In spite of these dissatisfactions, however, few of the women had sought or achieved. changes in their role as wives. The class and gender expectations of upper-class wives are largely taken for granted and accepted by them as a stable reality. One universal, if varying, reason for the acceptance is the presence of paid household help. Since the women are free of "mundane" household chores, the impetus to change their work as wives is considerably less than it is for other wives.

Next, I talked with the women about their responsibilities as mothers. They emphasized the importance of being personally available to their children, especially being at home when the children are small. They arrange their community volunteer work so they can be at home when the children return from school in the afternoons; and they turn down major or especially demanding outside responsibilities until the children are in the first grade. In general, they agreed that the task of raising the next generation is far too important to be done by others. For some of the women, as for other women, the demands of motherhood are somewhat burdensome and stressful. One woman spoke of feeling cut off from her friends and community activities since the birth of her two-year-old. Another looked forward to the years when her last child would be in school and she would have the day to herself.

When asked what they want most for their children, the women typically expressed the wish that their children "be the best" of whatever they chose to be. This personal choice, however, was quickly bounded by class expectations, which suggested tension between individual and class standards that the women themselves apparently did not see.

Upper-class mothers also want their children to make a significant contribution to society, to develop serious and disciplined interests in leisure and play activities, and to stay out of trouble (or risk the withholding of family inheritances). It is important that the children attend private, upper-class schools and do well there. They should participate in class-exclusive recreational groups ranging from early dancing classes to the once-in-a-lifetime society debut. Finally, they should make "compatible" marriages, which the women defined to mean "class" compatible.

These are stringent expectations, and there is evidence of strain as the young people are channeled in demanding and clearly defined ways. Clues to their difficulties surfaced as the women talked about their own youth and the pressures they had felt living up to the standards their families had set for them. A number of them mentioned that their own children had objected to taking part in the society debuts, and that they, as mothers, had insisted their children do so. One woman spoke of the consequences of her son's behavior, which deviated enough from class standards for the family patriarch, the boy's paternal grandfather, to cut off the boy's inheritance. These are recognized tensions; but the need to uphold class standards from one generation to the next is of such importance that tensions do not seem to be a cause for concern or change. The women primarily want their children to repeat the patterns that they themselves experienced growing up.

Next, the upper-class club was described as an important aspect of upper-class life. The club provides a place to meet and spend time with friends; it is also a place where class boundaries are set and class imperatives acted out. This is a source of tension for some women: at the club, they can relax with people of similar backgrounds and values, but they also view the club as yet another necessary part of upper-class life. Some women describe club membership as a social obligation and, in many cases, a family tradition.

Upper-class women are expected to "socialize" as part of their way of life. Some of this socializing is part of the process that maintains the boundaries of the upper class. Acceptance into upper-class clubs is by invitation only. If one is not born into the class, one must go through a ritual of becoming known and being sponsored for membership. Participation in this process, for most of the women, means serving as sponsors; those women in my sample who were newcomers had themselves, been sponsored. As with the other expectations of their class, the women accept their club activities as a required part of upper-class life.

Finally, I talked with the women about their work as community volunteers serving on the boards of major arts, charitable, and educational organizations. All of the women are involved in volunteer work, and most of them see significant personal advantages to such work. Their training in the Junior League presents them with opportunities to assume positions of leadership and influence. As volunteers, they are able to "direct policy and procedure and get involved in the power structure." This is true even though the women recognize that the men of their class, as previous studies

143

have shown,[1] have more power in these community organizations. As further evidence of their satisfaction with volunteer work, the women expressed the opinion that they are not only *better off* than paid workers, but they are *better* workers. They consider paid workers to be less responsible and less committed to their work; and they feel that paid workers do no more than what is required of them, while volunteers do more than is expected.

As with the other three roles, however, there is evidence of tension in the role of community volunteers. A number of women, some of whom are quite active as volunteers, see distinct disadvantages to volunteer work. Some are personally frustrated by the "emptiness" of volunteer work, which they see as "busywork," a symbolic gesture rather than a substantive contribution to the community's needs. Nearly half of the women I interviewed wish that they had obtained more practical educations enabling them to qualify for paid work, or they wish that they had worked in some paid capacity before their marriages.

Overall, however, community volunteer work offers more stability and less tension and stress than their other roles. The women's role as community volunteer is something of a locus for resolving the tensions of the women's other roles. Volunteer work is one way to avoid or resolve the possible conflict between the role of wife and mother and a role in the larger community. The flexibility of volunteer work allows the women to carry out their activities at home in ways that more demanding and rigid paid jobs would not. Their comments might have been made by women of any social class. They questioned what to do with a sick child when one has to be on the job, and how to care for the household and children when their husbands are away from home. It is evident that volunteer work allows upper-class women to continue in their current roles as wives and mothers; it also offers them a degree of personal satisfaction, independence, and accomplishment. Because of these personal rewards, they are not as likely to challenge the class and gender expectations of marriage and motherhood as women of other classes.

It appears that none of the personal tensions of the four roles of upper-class women—wife, mother, club member, and community volunteer—are sufficient to cause them to seek significant changes in these roles. The women typically resolve conflicts between individual choice and class gender expectations in favor of the expectations. These conflicts are not likely, then, to serve as a potential force for change. Further understanding of this absence of the potential for change can be found in a look at the social structural arrangements from which these demands derive, the social organization of class and gender.

Interactions and Contradictions at the Societal Level

As the previous discussion suggests, there are some aspects of upper-class women's lives that are not fully explained within a class context that can be better explained within the context of gender. These include the women's accommodation of their husbands, the primacy of their responsibilities as mothers, and their subordinate positions on community boards. In these instances, class and gender interact to explain the women's lives. In addition to these interactions, class and gender also contradict one another at various points in the women's lives. As members of the upper class, these women are subservient to no one; as women, they are subservient to the men of their own class. To begin to see these interactions and contradictions more clearly, it is useful to look at the differences between what the women actually do in their various roles and what impact these roles have on the class structure. This line of thought distinguishes women of the upper class from women of other classes; and it distinguishes between their position as women and as members of the upper class.

Looking first at the activities of upper-class wives, one is initially struck with how similar they are to the activities of other wives. Upper-class wives, however, make a contribution to the social order that is quite different from the contribution made by women of other classes. This difference, I suggest, derives in part from the economic position of the men for whom the wives' tasks are performed.

When women stroke and soothe men, listen to them and accommodate their needs, men of every class (as Talcott Parsons knew)[2] return to the workplace with renewed energies. When women arrange men's social lives and relationships, men of every class are spared investing the time and energy required to meet their social needs. When women run the households and keep family concerns in check, men of every class are freer than women to pursue other activities, including work, outside the home. But upper-class women perform these tasks for men at the very top of the class structure. As upper-class wives, they "free the men to do business"; and for men of the upper class, this means running the economic and polit-ical affairs of society. It is in this way that upper-class women's activities as wives contribute to class maintenance. Supporting their husbands as individuals, they support and uphold the very top of the class structure.[3] In this way they distinguish themselves from women of other social classes.

Looking at the responsibilities of upper-class mothers, one notices that they, too, do not at first seem to differ greatly from those of other mothers. Yet, again, looking more deeply into these activities and their impact on the class structure suggests a difference between the role of upper class mothers and mothers of other classes. One begins to see again how class and gender interact. Each of the women's aspirations for their children is—as was shown—either class-specific or class-oriented. But the aspirations of upper-class women—unlike those of other mothers—perpetuate the ex-pectations, special advantages, and privileges of their class. This occurs directly as a result of the work that the women do to construct and maintain, for example, class-exclusive recreational groups for their children. These groups, like invitational upper-class clubs, set the boundaries of the class and keep out those who are unacceptable. The women do the "dirty work" of deciding who gets in to these exclusive youth groups and, ultimately, to the society debut.

The role of the upper-class mother, like that of the upper-class wife, is defined within a particular class framework. This framework serves primarily to pass on, intact, to the next generation the life of privilege. The stability and dominant position of the upper class in society is thus due, in part, to the work performed by upper-class mothers.

Upper-class women's work as club members also has both class and gender aspects. For the men of the class, club activities may lead to business and political associations, thus supporting their dominant positions in economic and political affairs. For the women, the club is primarily a place to be with friends. But it is also a place where the class is constructed and carried on. The women, who are responsible for arranging the family's social life, arrange the social functions of the upper-class clubs as well. These functions create and maintain the relations that are the social fabric of upper-class life.

The women spoke, for example, of entertaining at the clubs; and one woman noted that she had met her husband there. These social relations build the solidarity and cohesion of the class. Other studies of the nation's class structure have noted that such solidarity and cohesion is unique to the upper class.[4] The clubs also serve as screening mechanisms for the class. Persons not born into the class are chosen by those who were to be club (and class) members. The process of becoming known and sponsored occurs through the "socializing" that is arranged by the women of the class. Again, the making of social arrangements, which is done by women of all classes to some degree, has a unique class function when done by upper-class women. It maintains the class as a social entity, particularly through the use of exclusive clubs.

The work of upper-class women as community volunteers does not have a direct counterpart in the lives of other women. It does have gender as well as class aspects. With some exceptions (such as women who are board chairpersons), the women I talked with believe they have less influence than the men of their class. The men run the financial affairs of the organizations; the women are more likely to be responsible for the day-to-day "service" activities. In contrast to these gender factors in doing such work, the reasons the women themselves gave are class-based. They do volunteer work to return some of what they have to the community, to carry on family tradition (since the organizations they serve on often were founded by their own families), and to oversee the organizations to whom they, and those they solicit from their class, contribute significant amounts of money.

These reasons for community work could not be given by members of any other class, and they clearly and directly maintain the class. As upper-class women share their energies and great wealth with those less fortunate, they also protect and justify those class privileges that they consider to be their "birthright" but that members of other classes may resent. As the women carry on family traditions of voluntary service and charitable contributions, they also carry on the class associations that dominate those organizations, on whose boards they serve and to whose coffers they contribute. As the women accept the responsibility to oversee the organizations for whom they raise funds, they also influence the policies and procedures of these organizations. For example, they keep client, consumer, and government representation out, and exercise influence over professional staff. A central aim of upper-class women's community volunteer work, as they describe it, is to keep private control over community organizations. Private control comes to be identified as the control of their own class. They exercise, explain, and legitimate such control through their economic power and their ability—because of their monied background and connections—to raise funds for the organizations.

In summary, it appears that there are inner tensions between personal choice and class gender expectations in the lives of upper class women; there are interactions and contradictions between the differential expectations and demands made of them as women and as members of the upper class. As wives, their activities are similar to those of other women. Yet the social meaning and impact of those activities are clearly class-specific and important for maintaining their class. Their class position as persons of wealth, influence, and status seems to conflict with their subservient relationships with their husbands. As mothers, their activities do not differ entirely from those of other mothers. Yet again, these activities take on a particular class meaning and consequence, which is primarily to pass on the life of privilege to the next generation. This is quite unlike the activities of mothers of other classes. As club members, upper-class women organize social and recreational life for themselves and their families, as do women of other classes. But their social life is the social life of a class, and their relations weave the fabric of upper-class life. As community volunteers, upper-class women work almost entirely as members of their class. They have little in common, here, with other women—except for the somewhat lesser degree of influence they have compared with the men of their class. Their reasons for doing such work are almost entirely class-based and hold little meaning for women of other classes. The consequence of such work is primarily class maintenance.

These societal contradictions and interactions, like the personal tensions discussed earlier, do not seem to hold within them significant potential for change. In each of the instances discussed above, there is more sense of stability in the women's lives—ordered as they are by both class and gender—than instability. Though tensions and contradictions are certainly present, their resolution is the more prominent feature of the women's lives. This resolution, I will next suggest, is primarily one of class.

The Overriding Class Context

In the women's conversations about their roles as wives and mothers, the gender aspect seemed most important to them in making sense of what they did and why they did it, though class was also very important. In discussions of their roles as club members and as community volunteers, the gender context was relatively unimportant. Their lives in these roles were defined almost entirely in the class context, with very little reference to gender. Indeed there was a striking contradiction between their descriptions of themselves as wives—clearly subordinate and deferent to husbands—and as club members and community volunteers—clearly dominant and not deferent to persons from any other class.

I found myself initially puzzled by the relative subordination of these women by upper-class men. Why do they allow themselves to be dominated, as women, by the men of their class? They have so much more of a basis for equality with these men than do women of other classes. They all have inheritances of some kind. They are not economically dependent on their husbands, at least not to the degree that other wives are. Why, then, do they not challenge their husbands' power at home? Why, particularly given their stated dissatisfactions, do they continue to be so accommodating to their husbands' needs and demands? Why accede so easily to the husbands' dominant influence in family decisions? Why do they give their husbands their family inheritances to manage—knowing that they are giving up an important basis for gender equality?

As I suggested in Chapter 3, there are several reasons why gender stratification is an accepted fact of upper-class life, virtually unchallenged by upper-class women. The simplest reason is that women—at least White women—of every social class are taught to believe that men are the major economic providers and decision-makers. The behavior of upper-class women is simply a variation of that traditional belief.

A second reason why upper-class women have not sought to change their traditional roles significantly is that their work roles, both inside and outside the home, are defined in part by class rather than gender. Upper-class women do not perform the nitty-gritty tasks of housework and childcare that women of other classes find so tiresome. They have others, typically women of other races and classes, do such work for them. Thus the impetus for change in the work role inside the home is considerably lessened. Furthermore, upper-class women do not need—economically, personally, or so-cially—to seek paid work outside the home. Economically they already have more than enough on which to live, and personally and socially they obtain sufficient satisfaction and sense of social identity from their volunteer work. Thus they are not subject to the long and rigid hours of work in the marketplace. Women of other classes—though they might prefer such work to full-time, unpaid work at home—are more likely to challenge traditional divisions of labor and inequalities at home.[5]

The main reason I want to suggest for the continued sub-ordination and deference of upper-class women to the men of their class is the economic and political position of upper-class men. In order to alter their subordinate position, the women, at this point in history, would have to challenge the power of upper-class men. These men dominate the economic and political affairs of the entire society. They know how to rule and are masters of the exercise of power. They are no more likely to be shaken in their positions as heads of their families than they are to be shaken in their positions as heads of society's economic institutions.

Furthermore, it seems not entirely in the best interest of these women to challenge the position of upper-class men, even if they could do so successfully. To do so would seem to challenge the very advantages of being upper class that the women spoke so highly of in the second chapter of this book. Those advantages continue to exist largely because upper-class men do dominate the economic and political affairs of the society. The women are very much aware of this. This interpretation is supported by the findings of this study that relate to the women's definition of upper class. These women are highly conscious of class. They have a genuine class analysis that they use to make sense out of their own lives, and they speak highly of the joys of their material standard of living and the freedom it gives them. They enjoy the pleasures of coming from well-known and well-respected families. And they appreciate the advantages of having direct and informal access to persons in positions of power who are their class, if not gender, equals. It may not, therefore, be completely in their best interest to challenge their gender-subordinate position, for to do so would seem to challenge the superiority of the class and the advantages that come from it.

Women of the upper class, especially married women with children, will most likely, therefore, continue in their traditional roles. They will do so in spite of the evident strains and contradictions of these roles. They will do so perhaps in part because the gains of *gender* equality would not be enough to balance the losses of *class* equality.

I began this study in search of the ways that upper-class women uphold their class, and the ways in which their activities are (or are not) given meaning within a class framework. I soon found it necessary to look more explicitly at gender as well as class for a more complete understanding of their lives.[6] I have shown how the women's activities uphold the class structure in various ways. It also appears that the class structure upholds the women's subordinate position. The position and activities of upper-class women support the continued dominance of the upper class; but this dominance—and the women's unwillingness to challenge it—supports their subordinate position.

I also began this study with the women's own descriptions of their activities and the meaning of these activities. The word meaning, here, refers to those institutional frameworks that exist in society that upper-class women use to make sense of their activities to themselves and others. Beginning with the women's experiences, I then looked further into the social structure, or framework, of their lives. This approach is particularly important at the beginning of a study of women, because women tend to have special responsibilities for the affairs of everyday life.[7] Indeed, it is possible to suggest that the activities of upper-class women integrate the activities of everyday life into the social structure of their class.

In this study, I have shown how upper-class women organize and interpret their activities primarily within the framework of class. In turn,—though they also interact with gender—these activities reinforce the objective existence of that class framework. Thus the lives of upper-class women create and are created by the class structure and, to a lesser extent, by the gender structure. For these women, the upper class is both the condition and the creation of their life activities; and their life activities are essential for upholding the class.

Appendixes
Notes
Bibliography

Appendix A
Description of Sample

Name	Approximate Age	Husband's Occupation	Social Register[1]	Most Elite Social Clubs[1]
Wainwright†	early 50's	Physician	–	–
Boynton	80's	Corporate Law	yes	–
Eton	50's	Investment Consultant (widow)	yes	yes
Bennett	80's	Corporate Law	yes	yes
VanHague	80's	(widow)	yes	–
Hall	late 40's	Business Consultant	yes	yes
Smythe	late 40's	Physician	yes	yes
Hoight	40's	Investment Consultant	yes	–
Ames	60's	Vice President, major old company	yes	–
Harper	40's	Partner in old law firm	yes	yes
Spears	50's	Corporate Law	yes	–
Vincent	40's	Treasurer of old major firm	yes	n.a.
Sharpe	50's	Stockbroker	yes	yes
Holt	50's	Purchasing Agent of old major firm	yes	–
Brownley	60's	Heads family philanthropic organization	yes	yes
Wilson	40's	Business Executive	yes	n.a.
•Hammond‡	50's	President of major firm	–	yes
Martin	60's	Corporate Law	yes	yes
Miles	60's	Chairman of Board of major bank	yes	yes
Howe	30's	President of small firm	yes	–
•Atherton	50's	President of large firm	yes	yes
Wright	70's	President of large firm	yes	yes
Lane	50's	President of old major firm	yes	yes

Number of Children	Junior League	Other Elite Clubs[2]	Children in Recreation Assembly[3]	Upper Class Girls Schools (Self)[1]	Upper Class Girls Schools (Daughters)	Upper Class Boys Schools (Sons)
	yes	yes (Garden)	n.a.	yes	(no daughters) (sons only)	yes
	n.a.	yes (Garden)	yes	yes	(no daughters)	yes
	yes	yes (Garden)	yes	yes	(no daughters)	yes (daughters only)
	yes	yes (Garden)	yes	yes	yes	(no sons)
	yes	yes (Garden)	n.a.	yes	yes	(no sons)
	yes	yes	yes	yes	yes	yes
	yes	yes	yes	yes	yes	(no sons)
	yes	yes	yes	yes	yes	yes
	yes	yes (Garden)	n.a.	yes	yes	yes
	yes	yes (Garden)	yes	n.a.	yes	yes
	n.a.	yes	yes	n.a.	yes	n.a.
	yes	n.a.	yes	n.a.	(no daughters)	yes
	yes	yes	yes	n.a.	n.a.	n.a.
	yes	n.a.	yes	n.a.	yes	yes
	yes	yes	yes	n.a.	yes	yes
	n.a.	n.a.	yes	n.a.	yes	(no sons)
	yes	yes	yes	n.a.	yes	n.a.
	n.a.	yes (Garden)	yes	yes	(no daughters)	yes
	yes	yes	yes	n.a.	n.a.	n.a.
	yes	yes	yes	n.a.	(no daughters)	yes
	–	yes	–	n.a.	(no daughters)	yes
none	–	yes	no children	yes	(no children)	(no children)
	yes	yes	yes	n.a.	yes	yes

Description of Sample (cont.)

Name	Approximate Age	Husband's Occupation	Social Register[1]	Most Elite Social Clubs[1]
Farley	40's	Heads family business	yes	yes
Appleton	40's	Business Executive	yes	yes
•Crowell§	30's	Environmentalist	(parents)	–
Carpenter	50's	Independent Business consultant	yes	yes
•Nesbitt	60's	President of major firm	yes	yes
Carnes	30's	Business Executive	yes	yes
Langdon	40's	Heads family firm	yes	–
Chambers	40's	Heads own investment firm	yes	yes
Cooper	40's	Heads wife's family's firm	yes	–
Haines	30's	Corporate Law	(parents-in-law)	yes
Garson	late 70's	(widow)	yes	yes
Clarke	30's	Partner family law firm	yes	yes
Hughes	50's	Chairman of Board of old major firm	yes	yes

n.a. = not available
– = negative instance
• = newcomer

[1]These three criteria for membership in the upper class were established by G. William Domhoff in *The High Circles*. I have purposely not used criteria related only to husband's characteristics, since it is the women's class and class origins that are of concern here. Domhoff considers the only one of the three criteria to be sufficient to establish class membership.

[2]In addition to the two social clubs Domhoff lists as being *sufficient* for upper-class membership in this city, he refers to a list of clubs compiled by Lucy Kaveler (1960). He considers membership in these clubs to be sufficient membership is compounded by one's father being a millionaire entrepreneur or a $100,000 executive or corporation lawyer (Domhoff, 1970, p. 26). Those subjects in my sample who belong to the "secondary" club (of which there is one in this city) are asterisked here. These women may belong to other clubs as well, particularly the city's oldest women's club. As noted, about a third of the women also belong to a garden club.

Number of Children	Junior League	Other Elite Clubs[2]	Children in Recreation Assembly[3]	Upper Class Girls Schools (Self)[1]	Upper Class Girls Schools (Daughters)	Upper Class Boys Schools (Sons)
4	yes	yes	yes	n.a.	yes	(no sons)
3	yes	yes (Garden)	yes	yes	yes	(no sons)
3	yes	yes	n.a.	n.a.	–	–
none	yes	yes	no children	yes	(no children)	(no children)
4	–	yes	recent resident	n.a.	n.a.	n.a.
3	yes	yes	yes	yes	yes	(no sons)
3	yes	yes	yes	yes	(no daughters)	yes
3	yes	yes	yes	n.a.	yes	yes
4	yes	yes (Garden)	yes	n.a.	n.a.	n.a.
2	yes	yes (Garden)	children too young	n.a.	yes	(no sons)
2	yes	yes	yes	yes	yes	yes
3	yes	yes	yes	n.a.	(no daughters)	yes
3	yes	yes	yes	yes	n.a.	n.a.

[3] The Recreation Assembly (not its real name) is listed by Kaveler (1960) as indicative of upper-class membership in this city. It is an invitational group for children and young people that leads typically to a debut at the city's most class-exclusive club.

† Mrs. Wainwright is a self-styled class rebel, and the daughter-in-law of Mrs. Boynton. Mrs. Wainwright had asked that her name be removed from the Social Register, and she turned down invitations to clubs.

‡ Mrs. Hammond and her husband—who heads a very large and important international firm—are relative "newcomers" to the city, having only been there 20 years. They are thus not listed in the social register and are not one of the old established families of the upper class. However, their daughter, Mrs. Carnes, is in the social register and is a member of the most elite upper class clubs.

§ Mrs. Crowell is a young woman who had moved some twenty miles outside the city to escape the pressures of her parents' class. She chose intentionally, therefore, to avoid upper-class institutions to which she had access, even to sending her children to public schools.

Appendix B
Interview Guides

Pilot Interview Guide (#1)

1. *Typical Day* (Entrance strategy: identify topics of interest and concern, expected and preferred activities)
   - What do you do on a typical day? Describe a typical day— yesterday, the day before, tomorrow.
   - Which of these activities do you find most/least enjoyable?
   - Which of these activities contributes to your own happiness or self-interest, to your family, to your community, to social concerns?
   - What motivates you to do those things which you find least enjoyable or of least importance?

2. *Ideal/Real Life Goals* (Values for self; self-reported behavior relative to values)
   - When you were twenty years old, what did you want most to do with your life? Have you done it? If so, what factors enabled you to fulfill this goal? If not, what factors made it difficult for you to meet your goal?
   - What would you like to be doing ten years from now? What do you think you actually will be doing? (Same question about aiding/inhibiting factors.)

3. *Socialization of Children* (Crucial measure of perpetuation of values of upper-class way of life and role of woman)
   - What important values do you most want your son(s) to learn? How do you personally go about teaching him these

values? What activities/groups is he involved in outside the family that reinforce these values?

- (Same question for daughters, noting differences and comparing with values of subject herself. Encourage subject to talk more about her own values and any changes in her own values, as evidenced in teaching children.)

4. *Awareness of Class Membership and Contribution of Women's Activities to Class Interests*
   - Would you say that you belong to an identifiable segment of a community whose values and activities are similar to yours? (If subject denies such class membership or does not speak in class terms, probe about origin of values and activities, presence of support group, reasons for not belonging.)
   - What other characteristics does this group share? (Ask about those obvious ones not mentioned, i.e., family background, husband's occupation, money, clubs, schools.)
   - Early in our interview, I asked you which of your activities you considered to be the most important contribution to your family and your community. How do your activities contribute, if at all, toward making your segment of the community a particularly influential one? What are your responsibilities, if any, as a woman member of this influential group? Are there ways in which you would like to exert your own influence as a member of this class? (*N.B.* The term "class" is used purposely at this late point in the interview to extract the subject's response to it.) (Ask subject for referral to another woman "of your group, concerns," etc.)

Revised Interview Guide (#2)

1. *Tell me about the activities you're involved in outside the home?* (If not mentioned, ask about volunteer work, social clubs and organizations.)

a. Which of these activities do you consider of most importance and why?

b. Which of these activities do you particularly enjoy? Are there any that you don't particularly enjoy? (e.g., most of us have to engage in activities we may not especially like for various reasons. Is that true for you?) Why do you think you continue in those activities you don't particularly enjoy?

2. *Tell me about your responsibilities at home.*
   a. . . . first in relation to your children. What, for example, do you want most for them in life? Consider the following:
      - values and life goals (definition of success)
      - behavioral expectations or norms
      - lessons, social clubs, entertaining of friends, extracurricular activities, summer work, travel
      - school (private/public)
      - most important characteristics of a good education (educational and social value)
      - occupation preferred for children (what about the girls?)
   b. . . . now let's talk about your responsibilities as a wife. Consider the following:
      - kinds of activities you do together with your husband
      - kinds of activities you're more likely to do separately
      - assignment of responsibilities at home. (For example, what is your husband responsible for at home? And you? What about hostessing, managing family finances and investments?)
      - wife's involvement with husband's work (For example, discuss problems)
      - important decisions (How were they made in the past?)
      - place of residence, schools for children
   c. Do you have other responsibilities at home that we haven't talked about?

3. *In general, do you find your life and activities at home and away from home to be satisfying?*
   a. Many of us would do some things differently if we had our lives to live over again. If you could be fifteen years old again, what might you do differently? What prevented you from doing that at the time?
   b. Are there things that you would like to do now that you are prevented from doing?

4. We've been talking about you, for the most part, as an individual. Now let's look at you as a member of the social group that I have called "old and influential families." What are some other characteristics of families like yours (e.g. money, place of residence, club memberships, private schools, tendency to marry and have friendships within the group)? How do you think the activities we've talked about help to maintain the somewhat unique position and influence of this social group?

Revised Interview Guide (Final)

INSTRUCTIONS: First, ask the general questions listed below, giving the subject an opportunity to respond in an open way. If a "typical" response does not emerge, note the "negative instance" category. Then ask specific questions—usually noted below as examples. (The testing of tentative hypotheses is based on twenty interviews to date.)

1. *Volunteer work*
   a. What are your current involvements in the community?
   b. What do you feel your own personal contribution has been through these activities? What has allowed you to be successful in this way? For example, to what extent have you been involved in fundraising?

163

c. What has it meant to you, personally, to be able to be involved in volunteer work? What would you have done if you had not had this option? For example, have you ever considered paid work?

d. What are the personal advantages and disadvantages to volunteer, as opposed to paid, work?

e. In your experience, how does the contribution of volunteers differ from the contribution of professionals? For example, do you see a difference in perspective?

- Some people have suggested that there is a trend toward using primarily professionals, rather than volunteers like yourself, to make the boards of various institutions. Would you oppose or support such a trend? Why?

- Do you think that you represent the community on the various boards on which you serve? Some would say that most board members like yourself represent the interest of a particular socioeconomic group. How would you respond to such a challenge?

f. What do you see as the major social problems in our community? Does volunteerism contribute to solving these problems? If so, how? If not, then what is the goal of volunteerism?

g. What do you think it would mean for the community not to have any volunteers? (Lead in to this question by citing the career interests of younger women, who will have less time for volunteerism.) For example, how do you feel about increased government involvement?

2. *Social Clubs and the General Issue of Exclusiveness*

a. To what clubs do you and your husband belong? (This is an objective check on class membership based on Domhoff's listing.)

b. What purposes do these clubs serve in your lives?

c. Why is it important that these clubs continue to be invitational? For example, the Junior League has, in the past few years, made its membership somewhat more open. Do you favor or oppose this trend? Do you think the League might, at some point, simply place requests for membership applications in the local newspapers? Why or why not? How would this change the character of the League? Would this be positive or negative in your view?

3. *Role in the Family*
   a. *Mother*
      - What do you see as your major responsibilities as a mother?
      - What do you want most in life for your sons? For your daughters? What does success mean to you for your children? What are the most important values that you want to pass on to them?
      - What activities have you encouraged your children to be involved in over the years? Why are these activities of importance to you?
        - Did your daughter participate in the Assembly Ball? Was it important to you that she participate in the Assembly Ball? Why, or why not? What would you have done if she had refused to participate?
        - What do you see as the main function of the Recreation League for boys and girls? Why is it important that this group continue to remain invitational?

4. What would cause the greatest problem for you in terms of your children? What would be the worst thing they could do? For example, how would you feel if a child of yours married someone of a different racial, religious, or social background? What would you do?
   a. *Wife*
      - What do you see as your major responsibility as wife?

- What are the main things that your husband expects of you?
- What are the main things you expect of him?
- Have your expectations of each other changed very much over the years? How?
- How do you and your husband divide up the work (economic support/running the house/child care)?
- How do you manage your personal and household finances? For example, do you have any money of your own? What has this meant to you?
- What would you and your husband consider to be a major decision (children's education, change of residence, job)?
- How have you helped your husband in his career? For example, has it ever occurred to you that your involvement in volunteer work might support his success or his standing in the community? How?

5. *Measure of General Satisfaction*
   If you had your life to live over again, are there any major things that you would do differently? If so, what?

6. *Measure of Class Awareness and Consequences*
   Do you feel that you come from a family of high social standing or prominence in the community? Why do you say that? What are the advantages and disadvantages to such social standing?

Notes

Chapter 1

1. The work of Dorothy Smith has been helpful to me in this formulation. See Dorothy Smith, "A Sociology for Women," in *The Prism of Sex: Essays on the Sociology of Knowledge,* ed. Julia A. Sherman and Evelyn Torton Beck (Madison: University of Wisconsin Press, 1977).

2. Anthony Giddens, *New Rules of Sociological Method* (New York: Basic, 1976), p. 158.

3. Objective measures of class are observable to the outsider and can be used to assign individuals to class groupings according to empirical criteria that exist in society. Subjective criteria are not directly observable and require judgment from the point of view of the subjects (those being categories). These "subjective" criteria—how the women themselves define upper class and give the concept meaning in their lives—are discussed in Chapter 2.

4. E. Digby Baltzell, *Philadelphia Gentlemen: The Making of a National Upper Class* (Glencoe, Ill.: Free Press, 1958), p. 60.

5. G. William Domhoff, *Who Really Rules?: New Haven and Community Power Reexamined* (Santa Monica, Calif.: Goodyear, 1978), p. 153.

6. Jonathan H. Turner and Charles E. Starnes, *Inequality: Privilege and Poverty in America* (Santa Monica, Calif.: Goodyear, 1976), p. 39; James D. Smith and Stephen D. Franklin, "The Concentration of Personal Wealth, 1922–1969," *American Economic Review* 64, no. 2 (May 1974): 162–167.

7. Bureau of the Census, U.S. Department of Commerce, *Statistical Abstract of the United States* (Washington, D.C.: The Department, 1981), p. 453; James D. Smith and K. Calvert Stanton, "Estimating the Wealth of Top Wealth-Holders from Estate Tax Returns," *Proceedings of the American Statistical Association* (Philadelphia: The Association, 1967–1972).

8. Domhoff, *Who Really Rules?*, p. 175.

9. Baltzell, *Philadelphia Gentlemen*, p. 7.

10. G. William Domhoff, *The Higher Circles* (New York: Random House, 1970), pp. 21–27.

11. W. Lloyd Warner and Paul S. Lunt, *The Social Life of a Modern Community* (New Haven, Conn.: Yale University Press, 1941), p. 118.

12. Baltzell, *Philadelphia Gentlemen*, p. 162.

13. Robert O. Blood, Jr., and Donald M. Wolfe, *Husbands and Wives* (New York: Free Press, 1960), p. 36.

14. Clarice Stasz (Stoll), *Female and Male* (Dubuque, Iowa: Brown, 1974), p. 193; Helen Mayer Hacker, "Class and Race Differences in Gender Roles," in *Gender and Sex in Society,* ed. Lucille Duberman (New York: Praeger, 1975), p. 138.

15. Paul M. Blumberg and P. W. Paul, "Continuities and Discontinuities in Upper Class Marriages," *Journal of Marriage and the Family* 37, no. 1 (Feb. 1975): 63–75.

16. Arlene Daniels has a forthcoming book on women and volunteerism entitled, *Invisible Careers: Women Community Leaders in the Volunteer World* (Chicago: University of Chicago Press).

17. Theodore Caplow, *The Sociology of Work* (Minneapolis: University of Minnesota Press, 1954), p. 265.

18. Joan W. Moore, "Patterns of Women's Participation in Voluntary Associations," *American Journal of Sociology* 66, no. 6 (May 1961): 598.

19. Helena Znaniecki Lopata, *Occupation: Housewife* (New York: Oxford University Press, 1971).

20. Ann R. Tickamyer, "Wealth and Power: A Comparison of Men and Women in the Property Elite," *Social Forces* 60 (Dec. 1981): 463–481.

21. Domhoff, *Higher Circles*, pp. 34–35.

22. Lucy Kaveler, *The Private World of High Society* (New York: MacKay, 1960); Cleveland Amory, *The Proper Bostonians* (New York: Harper & Row, 1947) and *Who Killed Society* (New York: Harper & Row, 1960).

23. Sociologist Arthur Vidich said in relation to field studies, "When the social scientist studies a society, he characteristically makes the first contact with marginal persons." See Arthur Vidich, "Participant Observation and the Collection and Interpretation of Data," *American Journal of Sociology* 60 (1955): 357.

24. Barney G. Glaser and Anselm L. Strauss, *The Discovery of Grounded Theory* (Chicago: Aldine, 1967).

25. Ibid.

Chapter 2

1. See, for example, Kurt B. Mayer and Walter Buckley, *Class and Society* (New York: Random House, 1970); Robert A. Rothman, *Inequality and Stratification in the United States* (Englewood Cliffs, N.J.: Prentice-Hall, 1978); Charles Hurst, *The Anatomy of Social Inequality* (St. Louis, Mo.: Mosby, 1979); Beth E. Vanfossen, *The Structure of Social Inequality* (Boston: Little, Brown, 1979).

2. For a more complete discussion of this point by the author see Susan A. Ostrander, "Upper Class Women: Class Consciousness as Conduct and Meaning," in *Power Structure Research,* ed. G. William Domhoff (Beverly Hills, Calif.: Sage, 1980).

3. W. Lloyd Warner and Paul S. Lunt, *The Social Life of a Modern Community* (New Haven, Conn.: Yale University Press, 1941); C. Wright Mills, *The Power Elite* (New York: Oxford University Press, 1956); G. William Domhoff, *The Higher Circles* (New York: Random House, 1970); M. S. Seider, "American Big Business Ideology: A Content Analysis of Executive Speeches," *American Sociological Review* 39 (1974): 802–815.

4. For challenges to this typical way of assigning women's class position see Marie Haug, "Social Class Measurement and Women's Occupational Roles," *Social Forces* 52 (Sept. 1973): 86–98, and Linda Burzotta Nilson, "The Social Standing of a Married Woman," *Social Problems* 25, no. 5 (June 1976): 582–592.

5. Though there were not enough "newcomers" in my sample to do an entirely separate comparative analysis, they will be referred to at several points throughout this study as having somewhat different experiences from women of the oldest upper-class families.

Chapter 3

1. Robert O. Blood, Jr., and Donald M. Wolfe, *Husbands and Wives* (New York: Free Press, 1960), p. 35.

2. Helen Mayer Hacker, "Class and Race Differences in Gender Roles," in *Gender and Sex in Society,* ed. Lucille Duberman (New York: Praeger, 1975), p. 138.

3. Lillian Breslow Rubin, *Worlds of Pain* (New York: Basic, 1976), p. 110.

4. Susan Kinsley, "Women's Dependency and Federal Programs," in *Women into Wives,* ed. Jane Roberts Chapman and Margaret Gates (Beverly Hills, Calif.: Sage, 1977), p. 80.

5. Andrew Cherlin and Pamela Barnhouse Walters, "Trends in the United States in Men's and Women's Sex-Role Attitudes: 1972 to 1978," *American Sociological Review* 46 (Aug. 1981): 455.

6. Rubin, *Worlds of Pain,* p. 176.

7. Joseph Pleck, "Men's Family Work," *Family Coordinator* 29, no. 4 (1979): 94–101.

8. Jessie Bernard, *The Future of Marriage* (New York: Bantam, 1972); Anne Locksley, "On the Effects of Wives' Employment on Marital Adjustment and Companionship," *Journal of Marriage and the Family* 42 (May 1980): 337–346.

9. Blood and Wolfe, *Husbands and Wives;* F. Ivan Nye and Lois W. Hoffman, eds., *The Employed Mother in America* (Chicago: Rand-McNally, 1963).

10. Hacker, "Class and Race Differences," p. 138.

11. Dorothy Smith, "Women, the Family, and Corporate Capitalism," *Berkeley Journal of Sociology* 20 (1975–1976): 80–82.

12. W. Lloyd Warner and Paul S. Lunt, *The Social Life of a Modern Community* (New Haven, Conn.: Yale University Press, 1941), p. 252.

13. E. Digby Baltzell, *Philadelphia Gentlemen: The Making of a National Upper Class* (Glencoe, Ill.: Free Press, 1958), p. 162.

14. Paul M. Blumberg and P. W. Paul, "Continuities and Discontinuities in Upper Class Marriages," *Journal of Marriage and the Family* 37, no. 1 (Feb. 1975): 75.

Chapter 4

1. Beth Vanfossen, *The Structure of Social Inequality* (Boston: Little, Brown, 1979), p. 296.

2. Paul M. Blumberg and P. W. Paul, "Continuities and Discontinuities in Upper Class Marriages," *Journal of Marriage and the Family* 37, no. 1 (Feb. 1975): 65–75.

3. G. William Domhoff, *The Higher Circles,* (New York: Random House, 1970), pp. 21–27.

4. Richard Sennett, *The Hidden Injuries of Class* (New York: Vintage, 1972); Lillian Breslow Rubin, *Worlds of Pain* (New York: Basic, 1976).

Chapter 5

1. See, for example, E. Digby Baltzell, *The Protestant Establishment* (New York: Random House, 1964); G. William Domhoff, *The Higher Circles* (New York: Random House, 1970). Baltzell says (p. 354) that upper-class clubs are "at the very core of the social organization of the accesses to power and authority."

2. Robert S. Lynd and Helen M. Lynd, *Middletown* (New York: Harcourt, Brace, & World, 1929) and *Middletown in Transition* (New York: Harcourt, Brace, & World, 1937); W. Lloyd Warner and Paul S. Lunt, *The Social Life of a Modern Community* (New Haven, Conn.: Yale University Press, 1941); August B. Hollingshead, *Elmtown's Youth* (New York: Wiley, 1949).

3. Kurt B. Mayer and Walter Buckley, *Class and Society* (New York: Random House, 1970), p. 87.

4. For further evidence that Jews are not accepted into upper-class clubs see Richard L. Zweigenhaft, "American Jews: In or Out of the Upper Class?," in *Power Structure Research,* ed. G. William Domhuff, (Beverly Hills, Calif.: Sage, 1980).

5. "Manner" not "manor" is the appropriate term here. The phrase comes from Shakespeare's *Hamlet,* Act 1, Scene 4.

6. Baltzell has been concerned that the upper class might become merely an exclusive status group with a "sense of caste." He sees this as a threat to the rights of power and authority of the class and quotes his arch antagonist Karl Marx to support his point. Marx wrote in *Das Kapital* that, ". . . the more a ruling class is able to assimilate the most prominent members of the dominated classes, the more stable and dangerous its rule." See Baltzell, *Protestant Establishment,* p. 3.

7. Domhoff, *The Higher Circles*, p. 79.

8. Baltzell, *The Protestant Establishment*, p. 354.

Chapter 6

1. I purposefully sought out women who were *not* community activists as well as those who were, since both types of women were mentioned to me by subjects as class equals. Having sought both types of women to interview, I found that being heavily involved was more typical than not.

2. G. William Domhoff, *The Higher Circles* (New York: Random House, 1970), pp. 39–41.

3. A number of the women I talked with thought that women younger than themselves and in some cases their own daughters would pursue paid careers.

4. Richard E. Ratcliff, Mary Elizabeth Gallagher, and Kathryn Strother Ratcliff, "The Civic Involvement of Bankers: An Analysis of the Influence of Economic Power and Social Prominence in the Command of Civil Policy Positions," *Social Problems* 26 (Feb. 1979): 298–313.

5. Ann R. Tickamyer, "Wealth and Power: A Comparison of Men and Women in the Property Elite," *Social Forces* 60 (Dec. 1981): 463–481.

Chapter 7

1. Richard E. Ratcliff, Mary Elizabeth Gallagher, and Kathryn Strother Ratcliff, "The Civic Involvement of Bankers: An Analysis of the Influence of Economic Power and Social Prominence in the Command of Civil Policy Positions," *Social Problems* 26 (Feb. 1979): 298–313; Ann R. Tickamyer, "Wealth and Power: A Comparison of Men and Women in the Property Elite," *Social Forces* 60 (Dec. 1981): 463–481.

2. Talcott Parsons, "Age and Sex in Society," *Essays in Sociological Theory* (New York: Free Press, 1954).

3. Dorothy Smith, "Women, the Family, and Corporate Capitalism," *Berkeley Journal of Sociology* 20 (1975–1976): 80–82.

4. See, for example, G. William Domhoff, *The Higher Circles* (New York: Random House, 1970).

5. Early evidence on this question suggested that once wives were employed outside the home, they would challenge the traditional division of labor inside the home, and they would gain more of a voice in family decisions. Studies such as the one by Robert O. Blood, Jr., and Donald M. Wolfe, *Husbands and Wives* (New York: Free Press, 1960), seemed to support that challenge; but more recent studies, such as Joseph Pleck's "Men's Family Work," *Family Coordinator* 29, no. 4 (1979): 94–101, seem less optimistic or, at least, equivocal about the possibility for fundamental change.

6. As a consequence of this study, I have become increasingly interested in the growing literature in feminist theory on class and gender. Useful sources include Patricia Caplan and Janet Burja, eds., *Women United, Women Divided* (London: Tavistock, 1979); Zillah Eisenstein, ed., *Capitalist Patriarchy and the Case for Socialist Feminism* (New York: Monthly Review, 1978); Heidi Hartmann, "Capitalism, Patriarchy and Job Segregation by Sex," *Signs* 1, no. 3, pt. 2 (Spring 1976): 137–169, and "The Unhappy Marriage of Marxism and Feminism," in *Women and Revolution,* ed. Lydia Sargent (Boston: South End, 1981); Annette Kuhn and Ann Marie Wolpe, eds., *Feminism and Materialism* (London/Boston: Routledge & Kegan Paul, 1978); Sheila Rowbotham, *Women's Consciousness, Man's World* (London: Penguin, 1973); Dorothy Smith, "Women, the Family, and Corporate Capitalism," *Berkeley Journal of Sociology* 20 (1975–1976): 55–89; Natalie Sokoloff, *Between Money and Love* (New York: Praeger, 1981); Eli Zaretsky, *Capitalism, the Family and Personal Life* (New York: Harper & Row, 1976).

7. Dorothy Smith, "A Sociology for Women," in *The Prism of Sex: Essays on the Sociology of Knowledge,* ed. Julia A. Sherman and Eveylyn Torton Beck (Madison: University of Wisconsin Press, 1977).

Bibliography

Acker, Joan R. "Women and Stratification: A Review of Recent Literature." *Contemporary Sociology* 9 (Jan. 1980): 25–39.

Amory, Cleveland. *The Proper Bostonians.* New York: Harper & Row, 1947.

_____ . *Who Killed Society?* New York: Harper & Row, 1960.

Anderson, Margaret L. *Thinking About Women: Sociological and Feminist Perspectives.* New York: Macmillan, 1983.

Babchuk, Nicholas, Ruth Marsey; and Wayne C. Gordon. "Men and Women in Community Agencies: A Note on Power and Prestige." *American Sociological Review* 25, no. 3 (June 1960): 399–403.

Bahr, Stephan J. "Effects on Power and Division of Labor in the Family." In *Working Wives,* ed. Lois W. Hoffman and F. Ivan Nye. San Francisco: Jossey Bass, 1974.

Baltzell, E. Digby, *Philadelphia Gentlemen: The Making of National Upper Class.* Glencoe, Ill.: Free Press, 1958.

_____ . "The American Aristocrat and Other-Direction." In *Culture and Social Character,* ed. S. M. Lipset and Leo Lowenthal. New York: Free Press, 1961.

_____ . *The Protestant Establishment.* New York: Random House, 1964.

_____ . *Puritan Boston and Quaker Philadelphia.* New York: Free Press, 1979.

Banaka, William H. *Training in Depth Interviewing.* New York: Harper & Row, 1971.

Barber, Bernard, and Lyle S. Lobel. "Fashions in Women's Clothes and the American Social System." *Social Forces* 31, no. 1 (Dec. 1952): 124–131.

Becker, Howard S. "Problems of Inference and Proof in Participant Observation." *American Sociological Review* 23 (1958): 652–660.

Becker, Howard, and Blanche Geer. "Participant Observation and Interviewing: A Comparison." *Human Organization* 16 (Fall 1957): 28–32.

Bell, Daniel. "The Power Elite—Reconsidered." *American Journal of Sociology* 64 (1958): 238–250.

Bernard, Jessie. *Women and the Public Interest.* Chicago: Aldine/Atherton, 1971.

———. *The Future of Marriage.* New York: Bantam, 1972.

———. *The Female World.* New York: Free Press, 1981.

Birmingham, Stephan. *The Right People.* New York: Dell, 1968.

Blood, Robert O., Jr., and Donald M. Wolfe. *Husbands and Wives.* New York: Free Press, 1960.

Blumberg, Paul M., and P. W. Paul. "Continuities and Discontinuities in Upper Class Marriages." *Journal of Marriage and the Family* 37, no. 1 (Feb. 1975): 63–75.

Blumer, Herbert. *Symbolic Interactionism: Perspective and Method.* Englewood Cliffs, N.J.: Prentice-Hall, 1969.

Bogdan, Robert, and Steven J. Taylor. *Qualitative Research Methods.* New York: Wiley, 1975.

Bruyn, Severyn. *The Human Perspective in Sociology.* Englewood Cliffs, N.J.: Prentice-Hall, 1966.

Caplan, Patricia, and Janet Burja, eds. *Women United, Women Divided.* London: Tavistock, 1979.

Caplow, Theodore. *The Sociology of Work.* Minneapolis: University of Minnesota Press, 1954.

Centers, Richard. *The Psychology of Social Classes: A Study of Class Consciousness.* Princeton, N.J.: Princeton University Press, 1949.

Chapman, Jane Robert. *Women Into Wives.* Beverly Hills, Calif.: Sage, 1977.

Cherlin, Andrew, and Pamela Barnhouse Walters. "Trends in the United States in Men's and Women's Sex-Role Attitudes: 1972 to 1978." *American Sociological Review* 46 (Aug. 1981): 453–460.

Coles, Richard. *The Privileged Ones.* Boston: Little, Brown, 1977.

Cramer, M. Ward. "The Leisure Time Activities of Economically Privileged Children." *Sociology and Social Research* 34 (1950): 444–450.

Dahl, Robert A. *Who Governs? Democracy and Power in An American City.*

New Haven, Conn.: Yale University Press, 1961.

Daniels, Arlene. *Invisible Careers: Women Community Leaders in the Volunteer World*. Chicago: University of Chicago Press.

Davis, Allison, Burleigh B. Gardner, and Mary R. Gardner. *Deep South*. Chicago: University of Chicago Press, 1941.

Dexter, Lewis A. "The Good Will of Important People." *Public Opinion Quarterly* 28 (1964): 556–563.

Domhoff, G. William. *Who Rules America?* Englewood Cliffs, N.J.: Prentice-Hall, 1967.

————. *The Higher Circles*. New York: Random House, 1970.

————. *Who Really Rules?: New Haven and Community Power Reexamined*. Santa Monica, Calif.: Goodyear, 1978.

————, ed. *Power Structure Research*. Beverly Hills, Calif.: Sage, 1980.

Eisenstein, Zillah, ed. *Capitalist Patriarchy and the Case for Socialist Feminism*. New York: Monthly Review, 1978.

Garfinkel, Harold. "Studies of the Routine Grounds of Everyday Activities." *Social Problems* 11 (1964): 225–250.

————. *Studies in Ethnomethodology*. Englewood Cliffs, N.J.: Prentice-Hall, 1967.

Giddens, Anthony. *Capitalism and Modern Social Theory*. New York: Cambridge University Press, 1973.

————. *New Rules of Sociological Method*. New York: Basic, 1976.

Gillespie, Dair L. "Who Has the Power? The Marital Struggle." *Journal of Marriage and the Family* 33 (Aug. 1971): 445–458.

Glaser, Barney G., and Anselm L. Strauss. *The Discovery of Grounded Theory*. Chicago: Aldine, 1967.

Goldstone, Bobbi. "Is She or Isn't She? Is Jackie Oppressed?" In *Marriage and the Family*, ed. Carol Perrucci and Dena B. Targ. New York: MacKay, 1974.

Gordon, Henry A., and Kenneth C. W. Kammeyer. "The Gainful Employment of Women with Small Children." *Journal of Marriage and the Family* 42, no. 2 (May 1980): 327–346.

Gordon, Raymond. "Dimensions of the Depth Interview." *American Journal of Sociology* 62 (1956): 158–164.

————. *Interviewing: Strategy, Techniques, and Tactics*. Homewood, Ill.: Dorsey, 1969.

Hacker, Helen Mayer. "Class and Race Differences in Gender Roles." In *Gender and Sex in Society,* ed. Lucille Duberman. New York: Praeger, 1975.

Hartmann, Heidi. "Capitalism, Patriarchy and Job Segregation by Sex." *Signs* 1, no. 3, pt. 2 (Spring 1976): 137–169.

——————. "The Unhappy Marriage of Marxism and Feminism." In *Women and Revolution,* ed. Lydia Sargent. Boston: South End Press, 1981.

Hatch, David L., and Mary A. Hatch. "A Criteria of Social Status as Derived from Marriage Announcements in the *New York Times.*" *American Sociological Review* 12 (1947): 394–403.

Haug, Marie. "Social Class Measurement and Women's Occupational Roles." *Social Forces* 52, no. 1 (Sept. 1973): 86–98.

Heilbroner, Robert L. *Marxism: For and Against.* New York: Norton, 1980.

Hiller, Dana V., and William W. Philliber. "Necessity, Compatibility and Status Attainment as Factors in the Labor Force Participation of Married Women." *Journal of Marriage and the Family* 42, no. 2 (May 1980): 347–354.

Hollingshead, August B. *Elmtown's Youth.* New York: Wiley, 1949.

Hollingshead, August B., Frederick C. and Redlich. *Social Class and Mental Illness: A Community Study.* New York: Wiley, 1958.

Hunter, Floyd. *The Community Power Structure: A Study of Decision Makers.* Chapel Hill: University of North Carolina Press, 1953.

Hurst, Charles. *The Anatomy of Social Inequality.* St. Louis, Mo.: Mosby, 1979.

Hyman, Herbert. *Interviewing in Social Research.* Chicago: University of Chicago Press, 1954.

Kavaler, Lucy. *The Private World of High Society.* New York: MacKay, 1960.

Keller, Suzanne. *Beyond the Ruling Class.* New York: Random House, 1963.

Kinsley, Susan. "Women's Dependency and Federal Programs." In *Women into Wives,* ed. Jane Roberts Chapman and Margaret Gates. Beverly Hills, Calif.: Sage, 1977.

Komarovsky, Mirra. *Blue-Collar Marriage.* New York: Random House, 1967.

Kuhn, Annette, and Ann Marie Wolpe, eds. *Feminism and Materialism.* London/Boston: Routledge & Kegan Paul, 1978.

Lampman, Robert. *The Share of Top Wealth-Holders.* Princeton, N.J.:

Princeton University Press, 1962.

Laumann, Edward O. *Prestige and Association in An Urban Community.* Indianapolis: Bobbs-Merrill, 1966.

Lenski, Gerhard, and John C. Leggett. "Caste, Class and Deference in the Research Interview." *American Journal of Sociology* 65 (1960): 463–467.

Locksley, Anne. "On the Effects of Wives' Employment on Marital Adjustment and Companionship." *Journal of Marriage and the Family* 42 (May 1980): 337–346.

Lopata, Helen Znaniecki. *Occupation: Housewife.* New York: Oxford University Press, 1971.

Lundberg, Ferdinand. *The Rich and the Super-Rich.* New York: Bantam, 1968.

Lynd, Robert S., and Helen M. Lynd. *Middletown.* New York: Harcourt, Brace, & World, 1929.

_____ . *Middletown in Transition.* New York: Harcourt, Brace, & World, 1937.

Mandle, Joan. *Women and Social Change in America.* Princeton, N.J.: Princeton Book Co., 1979.

Marx, Karl. *A Contribution to the Critique of Political Economy.* Chicago: Kerr, 1904. (Originally published 1859.)

_____ . *The German Ideology.* New York: International Publishing, 1947. (Originally published 1846.)

_____ . *Das Kapital.* Berlin: New Edition, 1953. (1st vol. originally published 1867.)

_____ . *The Communist Manifesto.* Chicago: Regnery, 1954. (Originally published 1848.)

_____ . *The Economic and Philosophical Manuscripts.* Trans. T. B. Bottomore. In *Marx's Concept of Man,* ed. Erich Fromm. New York: Unger, 1961. (Written 1844.)

Mayer, Kurt B., and Walter Buckley. *Class and Society.* New York: Random House, 1970.

Merton, Robert, and Patricia L. Kendall. "The Focused Interview." *American Journal of Sociology* 51 (1946): 541–557.

Michels, Robert. *Political Parties.* New York: Dover, 1959. (Originally published 1915.)

Miller, Herman. *Rich Man, Poor Man.* New York: Signet, 1968.

Millman, Marcia, and Rosabeth Moss Kanter. *Another Voice: Feminist Perspectives on Social Life and Social Science.* Garden City, N.Y.: Anchor/Doubleday, 1975.

Mills, C. Wright. *White Collar.* New York: Oxford University Press, 1951.

————— . *The Power Elite.* New York: Oxford University Press, 1956.

Moore, Joan W. "Patterns of Women's Participation in Voluntary Associations." *American Journal of Sociology* 66; no. 6 (May 1961): 592–598.

Morgan, Robin. *Sisterhood Is Powerful.* New York: Random House, 1970.

Mosca, Gaetano. *The Ruling Class.* New York: McGraw Hill, 1939.

Nilson, Linda Burzotta. "The Social Standing of a Married Woman." *Social Problems* 25, no. 5 (June 1976): 582–592.

Norton-Taylor, Duncan. "How Top Executives Live." *Fortune* 51 (1955): 78–169.

Nye, F. Ivan, and Lois W. Hoffman, eds. *The Employed Mother in America.* Chicago: Rand-McNally, 1963.

Ossowski, Stanislaw. *Class Structure in the Social Consciousness.* New York: Free Press, 1963.

Ostrander, Susan A. "Upper Class Women: Class Consciousness as Conduct and Meaning." In *Power Structure Research,* ed. G. William Domhoff. Beverly Hills, Calif.: Sage, 1980.

————— . "Upper Class Women: The Feminine Side of Privilege." *Qualitative Sociology* 1, no. 3 (1980): 23–44.

Pareto, Vilfredo. *The Mind and Society.* New York: Harcourt, Brace, 1935.

Parsons, Talcott. "Age and Sex in Society." In *Essays in Sociological Theory.* New York: Free Press, 1954.

Pleck, Joseph. "Men's Family Work." *Family Coordinator* 29, no. 4 (1979): 94–101.

Polatnick, Margaret. "Why Men Don't Rear Children: A Power Analysis." *Berkley Journal of Sociology* 18 (1973–1974): 45–86.

Poloma, M., and Garland, T. Neal. "The Married Professional Woman: A Study in the Tolerance of Domestication." *Journal of Marriage and the Family* 33 (Aug. 1971): 531–540.

Projector, D. S., and G. S. Weiss. *Survey of Financial Characteristics of Consumers.* Washington, D.C.: Board of Governors of the Federal Reserve System, 1966.

Rainwater, Lee, Richard P. Coleman, and Gerald Handel. *Workingman's Wife*. New York: Oceana, 1959.

Ratcliff, Richard E., Mary Elizabeth Gallagher, and Kathryn Strother Ratcliff. "The Civic Involvement of Bankers: An Analysis of the Influence of Economic Power and Social Prominence in the Command of Civic Policy Positions." *Social Problems* 26 (Feb. 1979): 298–313.

Reisman, Leonard. *Class in American Society*. New York: Free Press, 1960.

Rose, Arnold. *The Power Structure*. New York: Oxford University Press, 1967.

Ross, Alan. *Noblesse Oblige: An Inquiry Into the Identifiable Character of the English Aristocrat*. London: Hamish Hamilton, 1956.

Rothman, Robert A. *Inequality and Stratification in the United States*. Englewood Cliffs, N.J.: Prentice-Hall, 1978.

Rowbotham, Sheila. *Women's Consciousness, Man's World*. London: Penguin, 1973.

Rubin, Lillian Breslow. *Worlds of Pain*. New York: Basic, 1976.

Schuby, T. D., "Class, Power, Kinship and Social Cohesion: A Case Study of a Local Elite." *Sociological Focus* 8 (1975): 243–256.

Schutz, Alfred. "Common Sense and Scientific Interpretation of Human Action." In *Philosophy of the Social Sciences*, ed. Maurice Natanson. New York: Random House, 1963.

_____ . "Concept and Theory Formation in the Social Sciences." In *Philosophy of the Social Sciences*, ed. Maurice Natanson. New York: Random House, 1963.

Segal, Marcia Texler, and Catherine White Berheide. "Towards a Women's Perspective in Sociology." In *Theoretical Perspectives in Sociology*, ed. Scott McNall. New York: St. Martin's, 1979.

Seider, M. S., "American Big Business Ideology: A Content Analysis of Executive Speeches." *American Sociological Review* 39 (1974): 802–815.

Sennett, Richard. *The Hidden Injuries of Class*. New York: Vintage, 1972.

Shostak, Arthur B., Jon Vantil, and Sally Bould Vantil. *Privilege in America: An End to Inequality?* Englewood Cliffs, N.J.: Prentice-Hall, 1973.

Simmel, George. *The Sociology of George Simmel*. Trans. and ed. Kurt W. Wolff. New York: Free Press, 1950.

Smigel, E. "Interviewing a Legal Elite." *American Journal of Sociology* 64 (1958): 159–164.

Smith, Dorothy. "Women, the Family, and Corporate Capitalism." *Berkeley Journal of Sociology* 20 (1975–1976): 55–89.

—————. "A Sociology for Women." In *The Prism of Sex: Essays on the Sociology of Knowledge,* ed. Julia A. Sherman and Evelyn Torton Beck. Madison: University of Wisconsin Press, 1977.

Smith, James D., and Stephen D. Franklin. "The Concentration of Personal Wealth, 1922–1969." *American Economic Review* 64, no. 2 (May 1974): 162–167.

Sokoloff, Natalie. *Between Money and Love.* New York: Praeger, 1981.

Strauss, Anselm, and Leonard Schatzman. "Cross-Class Interviewing: An Analysis of Interaction and Communicative Styles." *Human Organization* 14 (1955): 28–31.

Tickamyer, Ann R. "Wealth and Power: A Comparison of Men and Women in the Property Elite." *Social Forces* 60 (Dec. 1981): 463–481.

Turner, Jonathan H., and Charles E. Starnes. *Inequality: Privilege and Poverty in America.* Santa Monica, Calif.: Goodyear, 1976.

Vanfossen, Beth E. *The Structure of Social Inequality.* Boston: Little, Brown, 1979.

Veblen, Thorsten. *Theory of the Leisure Class.* New York: Viking, 1931.

Vidich, Arthur J. "Participant Observation and the Collection and Interpretation of Data." *American Journal of Sociology* 60 (1955): 354–360.

Walker, Kathryn E., and William Gauger. "Time Spent by Husbands in Household Work." *Family Economics Review* 4 (1970): 8–11.

Warner, W. Lloyd. "Successful Wives of Successful Executives." *Harvard Business Review* 34 (1956): 64–70.

Warner, W. Lloyd, and Paul S. Lunt. *The Social Life of a Modern Community.* New Haven, Conn.: Yale University Press, 1941.

Wilensky, Harold, and Charles N. Lebeaux. *Industrial Society and Social Welfare.* New York: Free Press, 1958.

Williams, J. Allen, Jr., "Interviewer-Respondent Interaction: A Study of Bias in the Information Interview." *Sociometry* 27 (1964): 338–352.

Williams, Robin M., Jr. *American Society: A Sociological Interpretation,* 3rd ed. New York: Knopf, 1970.

Zald, Mayer N. "The Power and Functions of Boards of Directors: A

Theoretical Synthisis." *American Journal of Sociology* 75 (July 1969):
95–111.

Zaretsky, Eli. *Capitalism, the Family and Personal Life*. New York Harper &
Row, 1976.

Zelditch, Morris. "Some Methodological Problems of Field Studies."
American Journal of Sociology 67 (1962): 566–575.